TWILIGHT: LOS ANGELES, 1992

BY ANNA DEAVERE SMITH

DRAMATISTS
PLAY SERVICE
INC.

2

Ms. Smith dedicates this play to the memories
of her father, Mr. Deaver Y. Smith Jr.,
and her stage manager, Mr. Richard Hollabaugh.

GENERAL PRODUCTION NOTE

This is a form of documentary theater. It is a documentary theater piece about the Los Angeles riots of 1992. The riots occurred after a "not guilty verdict" at the end of a trial of four Los Angeles police officers who beat a black motorist, Rodney King, and were captured on videotape. This beating and the trial were national news in the early 1990s. An important part of the preparation for the play is thorough research about the events. The actors should be given a lot of research material, and possibly participate in the research. This play requires a different kind of acting than psychological realism and depends on an "informed actor."

This play is about a real event, using the words of real people. The audience should be made aware of that. Slides should be used, if possible, to announce each character and to inform the audience that the words in the play are verbatim from interviews. A slide with the following language should begin the show, just after lights down and before any other visual image:

"This play is based on interviews conducted by Anna Deavere Smith soon after the race riots in Los Angeles of 1992. All words were spoken by real people and are verbatim from those interviews."

The audience also needs to be given a background on the events. This can be achieved by the use of dramaturgical notes, but it can also be included in the body of the play — with visual aids, such as slides and videos if possible. The three most important videos to obtain are 1) the video of the Rodney King beating; 2) the killing of Latasha Harlins by a Korean shop owner; and 3) the beating of Reginald Denny, a white truck driver, by four black men. If the videos are not available, or if it is cost prohibitive to include them in your production budget, some other representation of these events is important. Based on the footage, the beatings could be staged or choreographed.

The actor's accuracy of language is important. All of the utterances, every "uh," is a rhythmic beat which informs the development of

4

character. Many times a character speaks in a counterintuitive way, in which words in and of themselves do not make sense. The play has been written as an extension of research done by the author on the relationship of language to identity. Language in this play creates identity, not from the words themselves, but from the actual arrangement of the words. It is recommended that a specific person be included on the production team who gives line notes and makes corrections. The process of playing the play, and speaking the words in their exact presentation, that will be another technique of acting.

Music and sound effects are useful and important for flow. Rap and hip hop music were an important part of the youth culture at the time. Music and sound effects are not included in this printed text, but there is a lot of room for the director to make decisions about how to use both. In all productions of the play performed by the author, original music was composed.

Costumes, stage sets and props can be as minimal or as ornate as one imagines. In all productions performed by the author, who performed it as a one-woman show, costumes were limited to pieces used for each character. It is important, however, that these pieces be as specific and individual as possible to avoid stereotype. Nonetheless, the costume designer has always been one of the more critical members of the production team. This play is about race relations and the degree to which we make assumptions about others based on the first visual impression they make. Costumes should be seen as an extension of that, with a mind to the fact that poor race relations begin with an inability to see the specific details of any person in front of you. In all productions done by the author, the set designers used the chairs of the individual characters as a way to assemble the staging. How a person sits tells us a lot about them, and a chair informs that. It is useful to think of all physical properties as functional, rather than decorative or indicative. What does the physical property allow the actor to do, in order to better portray the character, rather than how does it "look."

The play is performed in bare feet, except when shoes are meant to make a specific statement.

The play sees actors as cultural workers, who reach towards that which is "other" than themselves, to reach towards that which is different from themselves. To this extent, typecasting should only be used in relationship to casting which is about that reach for the other. The play is vocally and verbally demanding and requires first and foremost actors with a good vocal and physical range and a facility with language and movement.

The play also was created for nonprofessional, non "aesthetic" purposes. Inasmuch as this work is about a cultural "reach," the play can also be used with nonprofessionals who are interested in creating community and creating more vibrant work places, schools and towns in which difference of ideas and cultural background can prevail in a healthy way.

A film of the play performed and co-produced by Anna Deavere Smith is available through PBS broadcasting. It is meant as a reference for the acting technique and style of performance.

A NOTE ON CASTING

These characters are all real people who are alive or who have lived. It is not the intention of the play that any character be "sent up." The task for all actors is to suspend judgment and stereotype at all times. An actor is seen here as a culture worker meant to help society work on its problem with tribalism in a time that it prevails all over the world.

Some of them are in the public eye and can be researched. Their ethnic origin is very significant. It is essential. However, the ethnic origin is given not so that it will be replicated in casting but so the actor knows what they are working towards. The actor is performing the specifics of race and identity and working towards those specifics by paying attention to accuracy of language. Ethnicity, age, gender, class identity are all meant to be variables that the audiences sees shifting. The play can be played by all ages, from ten years old on.

If a character is identified as "black," it is not the author's intention that a black person play the role. If a character is identified as a "woman," it is not the author's intention that a woman necessarily play the role. It is possible to put together a company in which, at times, an actor plays his or her appropriate "type," but at other times, and most times, they do not. The idea of the play is to suggest that even in a volatile situation, where tribes, countries, cultures, races clash, it is important that some individuals have the ability to walk in the shoes of someone different from them, even an enemy. The theory of the play is that an actor has the ability to walk in another person's "words," and therefore in their hearts.

The play was originally created and performed as a one-person play. It is the author's intention that companies of all sizes, from one to twelve or more, play the play. To give an example of how identities can sometimes be accurate to race, gender, age and identity, here is a suggestion for a company of six. It is only a suggestion of how it could work. In the end, the strongest actors with the greatest vocal range and the greatest affinity for a character should play the parts.

Matching identities only becomes significant in the dinner party scene towards the end of the play, and sometimes to make a particular point, but each director will have an idea about this, as may the company of actors. The number six is chosen here, only because six is the number of guests at the dinner party. One could start there, in creating the cast, build the company around those characters/actors, and then move outward from that to cross-gender, cross-racial, cross-age casting. Age should not prohibit schools from doing the play. In a professional company, the use of adults and teenagers could bring an interesting diversity of age to the work, inasmuch as the play is about a younger culture and its confrontation of the establishment.

Again, these are suggestions, about what kind of identity switches could bring the most psychological and intellectual power to the development of a role. However, in the end, vocal, physical and verbal ability should prevail in casting decisions. Some of these characters require a lot of sheer vocal imagination and energy.

Suggested casting for a company of six

One Korean male
One white female
One white male
One Latino male
One black male
One black female

KOREAN MALE

Jin Ho Lee, Shop Owner
Hollywood Talent Agent
Chris Oh
Shelby Coffey III, Editor in Chief of the Los Angeles Times
Katie Miller
Gina Rae AKA Queen Malkah

LATINO MALE

Rudy Salas, Sculptor, Former Brown Beret
Elvira Evers

Maxine Waters
Federico Sandoval
Angela King
Joe Viola

WHITE WOMAN
Alice Waters, Chef, Chez Panisse, Berkeley California
Octavio Sandoval
Charles Lloyd
Jessye Norman
Josie Morales

WHITE MALE
Senator Bill Bradley
Cornel West
Keith Watson
Ted Briseno
Anonymous Juror
Reginald Denny
Twilight Bey

BLACK FEMALE
Elaine Brown, Former Head of the Black Panther Party
Elaine Young, Beverly Hills Real Estate Agent
Maria the Juror
Stanley Sheinbaum, Former President, Los Angeles Police
Commission
Walter Park
Mrs. Young Soon Han

BLACK MALE
Paul Parker, Head of the LA Four Plus Defense Committee
Jay Woong Young
Daryl Gates, Former Chief of Police Los Angeles Police
Department
Judith Tur
Mrs. June Park
Sergeant Charles Duke

9

This version of TWILIGHT: LOS ANGELES, 1992 was originally produced by Berkeley Repertory Theater (Sharon Ott, Artistic Director; Susan Medak, Managing Director) in Berkeley, California, on January 31, 1996. It was directed by Sharon Ott; the set design was by Christopher Barreca; the lighting design was by Pat Collins; the costume design was by Candice Donnelly; the sound design was by Stephen LeGrand; the original music was by Joshua Redman; the stage manager was Leila Knox; the assistant stage manager was Joseph Smelser; the assistant to the director was Karen Amano; the production assistant was Jennifer Marik; the assistant lighting designer was Alexandra Pontone; the resident costume design assistant was Cassandra Carpenter; the assistant sound designer was Lisa De Wolf; the assistant to the lighting designer was Elizabeth Chaney; the sound consultant was Gregory Kuhn; the voice coach was Judith Jablonka; the acting coach was Merry Conway; the video consultants were Avon Kirkland, Sam McKee and Evan Mower; and the slide consultant was Kevin Cain. It was performed by Anna Deavere Smith.

CHARACTERS

JESSYE NORMAN, opera singer, African American*

TED BRISENO, police officer, accused of beating Rodney King, Latino*

ANGELA KING, Rodney King's aunt, African American

STANLEY K. SHEINBAUM, former president, Los Angeles Police Commission, white, in his 70s*

RUDY SALAS, SR., sculptor and painter, Mexican American, in his late 60s

ELAINE YOUNG, real estate agent, Beverly Hills, white, in her 50s

CHARLES LLOYD, attorney, African American, in his 50s*

GINA RAE AKA QUEEN MALKAH, community activist, African American, 40s*

JAY WOONG YAHNG, former liquor store owner, Korean, heavy accent, 40s

JOSIE MORALES, clerk typist, city of Los Angeles; witness to Rodney King beating

SERGEANT CHARLES DUKE, Special Weapons and Tactics Unit, LAPD; use of force expert for the defense witness, Simi Valley and federal trials, white, well-built, 30s

ANONYMOUS MAN, juror in Simi Valley trial, white, late 30s

JOE VIOLA, television writer, white, 40s

KEITH WATSON, former security guard, co-assailant of Reginald Denny, African American, 20s*

SHELBY COFFEY III, editor, *Los Angeles Times*, white, patrician, 40's

KATIE MILLER, bookkeeper and accountant, African American, 40s

OCTAVIO SANDOVAL, occupation unknown, Latino

FEDERICO SANDOVAL, Octavio's brother, Latino

TALENT AGENT, anonymous Hollywood talent agent, white, 40s

ELAINE YOUNG, The Beverly Hills Real Estate Agency

JUDITH TUR, ground reporter *LA News Service* War Zone

DARYL GATES, former chief of Los Angeles Police department, white, well built, 50s,

ELVIRA EVERS, general worker and cashier; canteen corporation, black Pan American, 40s

CORNEL WEST, scholar, African American, 40s*

REGINALD DENNY, semi-truck driver; victim, white, 30s

PAUL PARKER, chairperson, Free the LA Four Plus Defense Committee, African American, well built, 20s

WALTER PARK, store owner, gunshot victim, Korean American, heavy accent, 50s

CHRIS OH, medical student, stepson to Walter Park, Korean American, no accent, 30s

MRS. JUNE PARK, wife of Walter Park, Korean American, heavy accent, 50s

MAXINE WATERS, congresswoman

ALICE WATERS, chef, Chez Panisse restaurant, Berkeley, CA, white, 40s*

JIN HO LEE, Korean American, macho, 30s, heavy accent

ELAINE BROWN, former head of the Black Panther Party, African American, light-skinned, 40s*

12

BILL BRADLEY, senator, D-New Jersey, white, 40s*

MARIA, juror #7, African American, 30s

MRS. YOUNG-SOON HAN, former liquor store owner, Korean American, 40s, heavy accent

TWILIGHT BEY, organizer, Gang Truce, African American, early 30s, late 20s, crips gang.

* All of these characters are available in news and video archives, as they have been in the public eye

TABLE OF CONTENTS

ACT ONE

ACT TWO

TWILIGHT: LOS ANGELES, 1992

ACT ONE

SLIDE AT BEGINNING OF PLAY

This play is based on interviews conducted by Anna Deavere Smith soon after the race riots in Los Angeles of 1992. All words were spoken by real people and are verbatim from those interviews.

ONCE UPON A TIME

JESSYE NORMAN
Opera Singer

Humming Tunes

*On a large, beautiful, British-made ottoman, wearing a color-
ful headwrap and rings, sipping tea.*

I sang, you know, as soon as I was able to speak, as far as I …
And my brothers kid me now,
they said "Soon,
we are going to read somewhere that you were singing in the womb.
Every time you talk about this it gets earlier and earlier"
But I was singing by the time I was able to speak,
humming tunes, and sort of doing stuff like that.
I just know that there were people
who would applaud if I sang.
And these people were in my own house!
And that,
my neighbor would call me across the street and say,
"You've got such a pretty little voice,
Why don't you sing something for me?"
And I was content
to sit on her steps,
Mrs. Hubert was quite old,
and she'd say "Well sing,
sing *Jesus Loves Me* you like that song."
And I'd sing it for her,
and she'd pat me on the shoulder and say,
"That was real pretty.

I like it when you sing."
And I would go home just as happy as anything.
I mean that was as good as
anything that could happen all day long.

TED BRISENO
Police Officer, Accused of Beating Rodney King

A Broken Heart

A thin man, not very tall, in cowboy boots and a wide belt.
Latino. Middle America accent. Empty stage. Walking.

But probably, the things that hurt the most —
was that
I wanted my children to look up to me
As their father
First,
but I wanted them to look at me as
as a hero.
I didn't have a hero,
when I was growing up.
I didn't have a father.
My father died when I was eight.
But I think it was a heart attack.
It's funny, cause back in the sixties,
you know everybody seemed like when someone died.
It was like heart attack,
heart attack heart attack, everybody was a heart attack.
My oldest sister.
She said, "Dad died of a broken heart."
Bein' older now,
I know what she meant,
by a broken heart.
And he couldn't provide the way he would have like to have
I just you know,
to this day it's still in the back of my head.
was that he died of a broken heart.
(Pause.)

So I grew up *(Louder.)*
basically without a father.
I had an older brother.
He went into the military.
I remember when I saw him in that uniform.
To me God that to me,
That was meant a lot.
I mean Wow.
Look at all those buttons and all those ribbons!"
And ...
And *(Louder.)*
because
being from a little small farmin' town I never seen something like that!
You know,
the local police,
didn't ya know,
It wasn't a real sharp type,
nice dress: your tie, your gig, your lines are straight,
your gunbelts zis *(sic)* nice and shine
your shoes.
Ya know, it wasn't anything
like
like out here,
or your big metropolitan cities where you look sharp.
But his uniform ...
It was impressive.

ANGELA KING
Rodney King's Aunt

Hand Fishin'

*On a high stool, in her studio and store in Pasadena, CA,
where she makes dolls and paints T-shirts. An African-
American woman in her forties in a pretty shirt, or kaftan,
smoking "More" cigarettes — long, thin, brown cigarettes.*

Things that we did,
like goin' fishin' …
I ain't never seen nothing like it in my life.
Rodney was down in the water had his
pants rolled up
feet and all
like these Africans,
done caught him a big old
(what do you call them things?)
trout!
By his
with his hands!
"I got him! I got him!
I got a big … "
'Bout that big
(She gestures, a big fish.)
I said "Boy! You sure you ain't got some
African in you?"
Ooh.
Yeah I'm talking about them wild Africans!
Not one them well raised ones,
like with a fish hook?
But to see somebody down in the water with the pants rolled up
like this here!

I said "Get out of there. You scarin' 'em you scarin' 'em!"
"Naw I got this one I got this one!"
Oh My God! Hand fishin'!
(She laughs a little uncontrollably at the memory.)
He was the only one I saw down in there in that water,
him and this other guy this big Mexican guy,
Sam?
I ain't never seen nobody fish with their hands!
Talkin' 'bout, "I ain't got time to wait!"
That's why I call him greedy
I wanted to ask him does he remember that.
He oughta remember it he was 'bout sixteen or seventeen years old.

SMOKE

STANLEY K. SHEINBAUM
Former President, Los Angeles Police Commission

These Curious People

A white man in his seventies, in a suit jacket. Brooklyn, Bronx like accent, tying a bow tie, as he speaks. Wedding ring. Standing.

Very
interesting thing happened.
Like a week and a half *(Very thoughtfully trying to remember.)*
Maxine Waters* calls me up —
You know who she is?
We're very good friends —
she calls me up and she says,
"Ya gotta come with me.
I been going down to Nickerson Gardens
and
the cops come in and break up these gang meetings … "
And these are gang meetings
for the purposes of truces …
(The author was momentarily distracted.)
Pay attention! *(Short laugh.)*
The next Saturday afternoon,
the next day even,
I go down with her,

* *Referring to congresswoman Maxine Waters.*

25

uh,
to,
uh,
Nickerson Gardens
(An abrupt stop, and second pause, as if he's forgotten something for a moment.)
and I see a whole bunch of, uh,
police cars,
sirens and the lights
and I say, "What the hell's going on here?"
So sure enough, I pull in there
(Three-second pause.)
We pull in there
and, uh,
I ask a cop "What's going on?"
and he says,
"Well, we got a call for help."
There's a gang meeting over there.
There's a community park there and there's a *gym*
and I go down to the ...
We go down to the gang meetin'
and half of 'em
outside of the
gym
and half of 'em
inside.
And here's about a hundred cops lined up over *here*
and about another hundred
over *here*
and, uh,
I go
into the, uh,
into the group of gang members who were outside.
Even Maxine got scared by this.
I gotta tell you I was brought up in Harlem.
I just have a feel for what I can do and what I can't do
and I did that.
And I spent about

two, two
hours talkin' to these guys.
Some of these guys were ready to kill me
(A bird chirps loudly.)
I'm the police commissioner,
and therefore a cop!
And therefore all the things that went along with being a cop!
It was a very interesting experience, God knows.
One guy who was really disheveled and disjointed
and disfigured
opens up his whole body
and it's clear he's been shot across ...
not in that ... not in that day,
months or years before,
and, you know
these guys have been through the wars down there
and;
You know, I hung around long enough that I could talk to them,
get some insights.
But the cops were mad,
they were really *mad*
that I would go talk to *them*
(Pointing towards the "gang members.")
and not talk to *them*
(Pointing towards "the cops.")
and I knew that if I went and talked to them
I'd have bigger problems *here*
But I *also* knew as I was doing this,
I knew *they* were gonna be pissed.
Two days I get a letter
and I was ...
the letter really pleased me in some way.
It was very respectful.
"You-went-in-and-talked-to-our-enemy."
Gangs are their enemy.
And so
I marched down to Seventy-seventh *(Precinct.)*
and, uh,

I said, "Fuck you,
I can come in here
anytime I want and talk to you."
Yeah, at roll call.
I said, uh
"This is a shot I had at talkin'-to-these-curious people,
about whom I know nothing!
And I wanna learn!
Don't you want me to learn about 'em?"
You know, that kind of thing.
At the same time, I had been on this *kick,*
as I told you before, of ...
of fighting for what's right for the cops,
because they haven't gotten what they should.
I mean, this city has abused both sides.
The city has abused the cops.
Don't ever forget that.
If you want me to give you an hour on that, I'll give you an hour on
that.
Uh,
and at the end,
uh,
I knew I hadn't won when they said,
"So which side are you on?"
When I said, I said, it's ...
my answer was
"Why do I have to be on a side?"
Yu, yuh, yeh know.
"Why do I have to be on a side?
There's a problem here!"

RUDY SALAS, SR.
Sculptor and Painter

My Enemy

*A Mexican-American man, in his sixties. Jeans. Simple shirt,
at a table in his living room, with a plastic tablecloth. Huge
plastic bottle of Pepsi and glass. His wife in the background.
He is seated, but gets up from time to time as he speaks.
Eyeglasses. Very subtle slight accent, more L.A. than Mexican,
but the suggestion is there.*

And then my
my grandfather
N Carnacion!
Uh
was a
gringo hater!
Cause he had run-ins with gringos,
when he was riding.
He had been a rebel!
So see, there was another twist!
He had rode with Villa and those people and he remembers when
he fought the gringos when they
went into Chihuahua.
Pershing went in there to chase Villa and all that?
So I grew up with all this rich stuff at home —
(Three quick hits on the table and a double sweep.)
And then at school
first grade, they started telling me
I was inferior
because I was a Mexican!
And that's where,
I knew from an early age

(He hits the table several times, taps, twenty-three taps until line "my enemy" and then on "nice white teachers" his hands sweep the table.)
I realized I had an enemy
and that enemy-was-those-nice-white-teachers.
I wonder what it is?
Why?
Did I have this madness?
That I understood this?
It's not an enemy I hated!
It's not a hate thing!
The insanity that I carried with me, started when I took the beating
from the police.
Okay that's where the insanity came in.
In forty-two
when I was in my teens!
Running around as a zootsuiter!
One night, cops really tore me up bad!
One of them said something about my mama!
I turned around, I threw a punch at one of 'em!
I didn't hit him hard!
But that sealed my doom!
They took me to a room —
and they locked the door behind me!
And there was four guys four cops there,
kicking me in the head!
As a result of the kicks in the head, they fractured my eardrum!
And uh
I couldn't hear!
On both ears!
I was deaf,
worse than I am now!
(He pulls out one of his hearing aids.)
So
from that day on,
I I had a hate in me.
Even now,
I don't like to hate, never do,
the way that my Uncle Abraham told me that to hate, is to waste

energy and you mess with the man upstairs.
I used to read the paper it's awful! It's awful!
If I would read about a cop, shot down in the street!
Killed!
Dead!
A human being!
A fellow human being?
I say
"So you know you know, so what?
Maybe he's one of those motherfuckers that
y'know ... "
I'm hooked on the news at six and the newspapers
and every morning I read injustices!
And poor Margaret has to put up with me.
'cause I rave and I rant and I walk around here —
I gotta eat breakfast over there,
I can't eat breakfast with her,
'cause I tell her
"These goddamned peckerwoods!"
So she puts me out there,
but I don't hate rednecks and peckerwoods
And when I moved in here,
it's all peckerwoods.
I had to put out my big Mexican flag out of my van!
Oh heck
I got my pride!
I told my kids a long time ago fears that I had,
not physically inferior
(Responding to the author.)
N t a physical fear,
not a physical fear.
That's the o...er tl .ng!
I grew up with the idea that
Whites, are *(Pause.)*
Physically ...
I still got that see that's a prejudice
that whites are physically *(Pause.)* ... inferior,
physically afraid of minorities

People of color, blacks, and Mexicans.
It's a physical thing.
It's a mental, mental thing that they're physically afraid
I I can still see it!
I can still see it!
And and
and uh uh,
I love to see it!
It's just how I am!
I can't help myself when I see
the right
person,
do the right thing.
If I see the right white guy
or the right,
Mexican walk down the mall —
(He makes a face and laughs.)
And the whites
you know they go into their thing already *(He mocks fear.)*
But you see I still have that prejudice against whites
(But.) I'm not a racist!
But I have white friends though!
But I don't even see them as whites!
I don't even see them as whites!
And my boys …
I had a lot of anxiety
I told them
"Cooperate man!
something happens
your hands …
(Puts his hands up.)
let them call you what they want!
Be sure tell me who they are!"
But they never told me!
My oldest son Rudy will tell you about it
Didn't they,
Margaret
insult him one time and they pulled you over

the Alhambra cops they pulled you over
and aww man ...
My enemy!

ELAINE YOUNG*
Real Estate Agent

Safe and Sound in Beverly Hills

A white woman who has had thirty-six plastic surgeries. Platinum blond hair. Jewelry. Flashy, expensive, designer glasses. At her desk in her Beverly Hills office. Fancy frames, accessories, a phone, a paper cup of coffee in a bag with Sweet and Lows. Manicured.

God it's so awful to tell somebody
when they wanna know what people thought of their house
(She puts the speaker phone on by hitting the button with a silver-plated pen)

JEFFREY *(V.O., British accent.)*

Hello?

ELAINE

Jeffrey?

JEFFREY *(V.O.)*

Elaine! Good morning!

ELAINE *(Sounding depressed.)*

Good morning.

There is an image of Elaine Young in the first five minutes of the PBS film version of Twilight, *a blond woman in a navy blue shirt.*

34

JEFFREY

How *are* you?

ELAINE

I'm okay *(A little sad.)*
I hate reporting back to you that people
are not interested in your house though.

JEFFREY

Listen.
If they're not interested what can we do?
They came and they *saw*
we didn't conquer
but they came and they *saw.*

ELAINE

But I'm coming up tomorrow
and that will be
eleven.

JEFFREY

Oh good!

ELAINE

I love you.

SHE HANGS UP

Oh I just love him!
This guy,
manages
Joan Collins,

George Hamilton,
Raquel Welch,
Linda Grey, everybody.
He's getting all of their houses.
He is so good to me,
and he
is so difficult.
Anyway …
Let's Go!
(In response to question by the author.)
You can repeat whatever I say
I mean I will tell you *exactly*
Twenty-ninth of April, was that a Wednesday?
Thursday?
Did you hear what happened to me because of being at the Beverly
Hills Hotel?
I don't know if you know,
but I do a lot of publicity and a lotta television,
all the time
I mean I do
shows on real estate and shows
on silicone.
I mean they call me to Washington,
I did
I been on *Sixty*
Minutes.
I've had silicone injections and I had
thirty-six surgeries on my face.
I'll show you
this is some of the PR that
I do.
(She takes out a large photo album, fancy book, leather bound.)
I started the fight for silicone
making it illegal
A lot of interviews
and they interviewed me when the hotel closed because I ate lunch
there
every day for thirty-six years

or I ate lunch there for thirty-six years.
But apparently
and I'm diversing [sic].
And I was also married to Gig Young,
and there was a big scandal
and then they wrote a book about him.
So they interviewed me for that.
So when they call me to interview me.
I'm never sure what it's gonna be for,
whether it's real estate,
which I love to do.
Silicone I do to help other people *(She claps her hands.)*
because
I was such a victim!
I was paralyzed for one year.
My face was like this,
and my eye was like that.
They removed grapefruit sized silicone,
from my face.
They went and drilled a hole in my head,
went into my bone and put bone marrow here.
I've had eighteen surgeries on this eye. *(Points.)*
This was *(Pointing.)*
a fifteen-hour surgery I almost died.
And uh
I just said what can I give back to the world
Because of what?
All I had was injections to give me cheekbones nothing more!
You'll read the story.
And so I decided I would do interviews to keep women,
and men,
from having silicone injected in their bodies,
it belongs in cars!
And so, I went on this crusade in between my work,
so I'm used to doing television.
I'm pretty good.
And I would never hurt anybody, do anything wrong.
But apparently,

when I did the interview it didn't come out right.
You know sometimes things are taken out of context.
And then I'll tell you what happened on Thursday.
Well maybe I should lead up to it to explain why I said what I did
and how frightened,
Why I was so frightened.
Oh
the day of the riot,
we were sitting here safe and sound in Beverly Hills,
and it was
like
one-thirty
two o'clock,
'cause it was starting slowly and building
people started yelling in the office
"Look out the window!
We see smoke!"

NO JUSTICE NO PEACE:
THE STORY OF LATASHA HARLINS

CHARLES LLOYD
Attorney for Soon Ja Du

An impeccably dressed black man in his late forties, early fifties. His office is filled with accoutrements — two red boxing gloves in a case, fine furniture, very neat desk, with expensive accessories. He is standing in front of a television, holding a remote. He pushes the button on his phone and speaks into it. Deep vocal register, good resonance and impeccable diction. He speaks quickly, nonstop. You can tell he's effective with a jury.

Note: For Dramaturg or Director: on the story of Latasha Harlins.

Latasha Harlins was a young black girl who was shot down by a Korean shop owner, Mrs. Soon Fa Du. The facts are contested by both communities. For those on the side of Mrs. Du, Latasha was stealing orange juice and beating Mrs. Du with a chair; for those on the side of Harlins, Du shot her in the back over a carton of orange juice which Latasha had no intention of stealing. The judge's sentence was very light and many interpret the violence against Korean Americans during the riot that followed the Rodney King trial — as a reaction to the Harlins case, which was on trial one year before the King case. The trial was covered in Los Angeles newspapers.

The actual video footage of the shooting of Latasha Harlins is available and is shown here.

Barbara!
Would you get me the coroner's report, please?
(Turning the television video on.)
Latasha hits Mrs. Du in the face four times,
very viciously,
and knocks her down twice.
I mean, this fight was no contest.
I'll take the girl.
I'll take the girl.
This *little* girl,
And didn't you think the girl was much smaller?
Misleading,
mis ...
she's five-six, one-hundred-and-fifty-two pounds,
and she *beat* the hell out of this lady
Now watch this very carefully —
This is an enhanced tape because it was a surveillance tape and it
was used over and over again
that's why it is such poor quality
It would have cost three hundred thousand dollars to get it any
better than this
*(This whole section is delivered with the speed, defiant efficiency of an
old-time professional radio boxing sports cast announcer. It is very fast,
nonstop and should feel like a real "feat of delivery." Fifteen seconds
from "Boom!" to "right in front of the cash register.")*
Boom! *(Hard, loud.)*
Looka there in the face
Boom! *(Hard, loud.)*
Latasha knocks Mrs. Du down, the lady throws the chair.
Mrs. Du reaches under the counter,
picking up a gun now!
Trying to take it out of a holster,
Latasha comes up to the counter with the orange juice!
just like Hollywood —
She puts the orange juice back,
and the gun,
the girl sees the gun.
Makes one step!

40

Boom!
Blood, brains all over, right in front of the cash register.
(Now it slows down.)
They had the girl walkin' out of the store.
But if you look at the girl's head in relationship to the cash register.
Right under there.
Thirty-six feet
from the front door.
Isn't that sad?
Isn't human life cheap?

GINA RAE
AKA QUEEN MALKAH*
Community Activist

African-American woman, very dressed up, with fingernails that are about five inches long, at a very simple, plain desk in a simple room.

We found it very unusual, that Charles-Lloyd,
The-top-black-attorney
In-this-city,
a millionaire,
would-take-this-case.
But for Charles Lloyd
To-defend-a-Korean-woman —
in the death of a black child …
I guess he just
Sold-his-card.
He's not a card-carrying member
of our community or of us
as-a-nation-of-people-any-longer.
He was a sellout.
I guess that's the best way to put it.
Because we all know, as we sit here
as black people,
if *any* of us had killt [sic] a Korean
child,
shot-them-in-the-back-of-the-head,
and it was recorded on videotape,
we-would-not-be-sitting-here-today.

* *There is an image of the real Gina Rae in the PBS version of* Twilight *at the beginning of the no justice no peace segment, identifiable by her fingernails.*

JAY WOONG YAHNG
Liquor Store Owner

*Korean man. Standing at the cash register in his grocery/
liquor store. Wearing a simple shirt, and large metal watch.
Heavy Korean accent.*

When Soon Ja Du took the gun
because so nervous,
so angry,
so angry,
that's only find the gun, that's why.
That's only two, three second.
Think about it.
Even if Natasha steal the money,
how could Soon Ja Du think
about …
why, she,
even if she's a steal the money or whatever,
how could she think about
shoot and kill her?
Soon Ja Du never experience not even the army,
she's like a good housewife
and mother.
Think about it.

CHARLES LLOYD
Attorney for Soon Ja Du

Again, a very verbal man, a gift for talking — speaking rapidly, with expression, an argument, a plea.

How am I sellout?
How am I an Uncle Tom?
A lot of this is just plain old jealousy.
I learned that as a child.
Whoever had the money in town.
Doctors, morticians,
It's like actresses.
People say that actresses are fickle!
I haven't found actresses to be any more fickle than anyone else.
And you have that going with lawyers.
"What looks good on a lawyer?
That's black and brown?
A doberman
A vicious doberman!"
"Why won't a snake bite a lawyer?" —
Professional courtesy."
"What does a lawyer do when he dies?
He-lies-still!"
Now this lady accosted a child for shoplifting
How is that a political case?
Let's read the ballistics report into the record.
"A hair trigger"
(He stops and responds to a question from the author.)
A hair trigger?
That's an expression from the Old West.
It's something men know a lot more about than women.
" ... external examination
has revealed evidence

of disassembly
the-wrong-screws-were-reassembled
dry-firing-of-this-weapon-reveals-that-the-hammer
can-be-pushed-off
without — pulling — the trigger!
Hitting the hammer in full cock
will discharge this firearm without pulling the trigger.
This firearm must be classified as
unsafe!"
They *made* it political!
If Latasha had been killed by a black woman it wouldn't have ever been
in the black the papers,
it's such a common occurrence!

GINA RAE
AKA QUEEN MALKAH
Community Activist

Now,
it might sound very racist on my part
and
I don't really care
at this point
if it does ...
Those Koreans all look alike,
little bitty short women,
with little round faces
and little short haircuts.
Soon Ja Du
coulda went and got on a plane
anywhere any day,
and nobody,
ever know the difference.
And so we said,
"Hey,
she-might-leave-here-today.
She needs to be in jail.
She needs to be in jail."
And we marched
and we started
"No Justice No Peace."

JAY WOONG YAHNG
Liquor Store Owner

You don't understand that situation!
Maybe I understand
because I have a similar situation in my store.
Five, six,
you know,
that youngster
like a fifteen, seventeen years old
that's usually black, black
guys.
And
they come,
you know, come inside,
at one time,
And one guy's talking with me,
one guy's
asking the price, and one guy's
asking which one is where.
That makes me,
makes me
pay attention the other place,
and they gonna try steal something!
They wear the big backpack
and they put inside something,
a soda, whatever.
After that I really *hate* this country.
I really *hate*.
We are not like customer and owner
but just like *enemy*.

GINA RAE
AKA QUEEN MALKAH
Community Activist

There were two children
who were eyewitnesses to Latasha's death.
And they both testified
that Latasha
begged Mrs. Du to let her
go and that she was not trying to steal orange juice
and Latasha lay dead with two dollars in her hand.
Her last act was two dollars in her hand.
If-the-white-media-does-not-decide-to-print-something-that
Happens-to-us,-we-won't-know.
That is another reason that I think we
have to travel the country and make it known.
Because justice denied Latasha Harlins
is justice denied every American citizen.
And the sentencing of Soon Ja Du,
was a five-hundred-dollar fine,
"restitution of the funeral
expenses."
You-can't-bury-a-dog-in-Los-Angeles-for-five-hundred-dollars.
Latasha's service cost seven thousand dollars.
So five hundred dollars' fine?
We think it's to the tune-of-one-billion
It-cost-the-city
April twenty the ninth [sic].
Because no matter what people say,
the injustice of what happened to Rodney King,
it just coincides,
as there's a parallel
between Rodney and Latasha.

THE STORY OF RODNEY KING
The First Trial/Simi Valley February 1992

The Rodney King Beating is shown here on video (available online: George Holliday* web site).

JOSIE MORALES
Clerk typist, City of Los Angeles
Witness to Rodney King beating

Indelible Substance

A small woman in her thirties. A feminine sweater. The interview took place in a government type office, sterile, no ambience.

We lived in Apt. A6,
right next to A8
which is where George Holliday lived.
And um
the next thing we know is um,
Ten or twelve officers made a circle around (Rodney King)
and they started to hit him.
I remember
that they just not only hit him with sticks,
they also kicked him,
and one guy,
one police officer even pummeled his fist
into his face.

* *George Holliday, a civilian, is the man who, by chance, had a video camera handy when Rodney King was beaten. It was he who made the video of the beating.*

And they were kicking him
and then we were like "Oh my goodness"
and I was just watching,
I felt like Oh My goodness
'cause it was really like
he was in danger there.
It was such
an oppressive atmosphere.
I knew it was wrong.
Whatever he did.
I knew it was wrong.
I just knew in my heart,
this is wrong,
you know they can't do that.
And even my husband was petrified
My husband said "Let's go inside,"
he was trying to get me to come inside
and away from the scene.
But I said "No"
I said "We have to stay here,
and watch
because this is wrong."
And he was just petrified,
he grew up in another country where this is prevalent
police abuse is prevalent in Mexico.
So we stayed and we watched the whole thing.
And
I was scheduled to testify
and I was kind of upset at the outcome
because I had a lot to say.
And I was just very upset,
and I um
I had received a subpoena
and I told the prosecutor "When do you want me to go?"
He says "I'll call you later and I'll give you a time."
And the time came and went and he never called me.
So I started calling him
I said "Well are you going to call me or not?"

And he says, "I can't really talk to you
and I don't think we're going to be using you because
it contradicts what the highway patrol said."
And I faxed him a letter
and I told him that those officers were going to be acquitted
and I told him:
If you do not put witnesses,
If you don't put one resident and testify to say what they saw
that those officers were going to be acquitted
but I really believe that the prosecution was dead set
on that video
and that the video would tell all.
But you see, the video doesn't show you where those officers went
and assaulted Rodney King at
the beginning.
You see that?
And I was so upset I told my co-worker I said "I had a terrible dream
that those guys were acquitted"
and she goes "Oh no, they're not gonna be acquitted,"
She goes "You, you,
you know, don't think like that."
I said, "I wasn't thinking, I had a dream
(Author asks a question.)
I just had this dream, and in my heart felt,
and I saw the
men
and it was in the courtroom and I just
had it in my heart
something is happening
and I heard they were acquitted.
Yeah, I do have dreams
that come true,
but not as vivid as that one
I said "Look at this
they were
they were acquitted
because dreams are made of some kind of indelible substance.
And my co-worker said "You shouldn't think like this."

and I said "I wasn't thinking!
It was a dream."
And that's all,
and it came to pass.

SERGEANT CHARLES DUKE
Special Weapons and Tactics Unit, LAPD, Use of force expert for the defense witness, Simi Valley and Federal trials

Control Holds

A handsome white man, very muscular, like a person who trains or lifts weights, large biceps — police uniform and police boots. He is showing the video of the Rodney King beating. There is a television on a rolling cart. There is a table downstage of him, with a policeman's baton, a pitcher of water and a glass: All of his movements are efficient and precise and clean. He starts by pointing the remote to the beating, then he pauses it.

Powell, holds the baton
like this
and that is
not a good
(He picks up a baton from the table and demonstrates)
the proper way of holding the baton
is like this.
So one of the things
they keep talking about—
"Why did it take fifty-six baton blows?"
The whole thing boils down to,
Powell has no strength and no power
in his baton strikes
because he was weak and inefficient with the baton training.
(He carefully pours water and drinks it.)
Oh I know what I was gonna do.
Prior to this
we lost upper body control holds

in 1982
If we had upper body control holds
involved in this
this tape woulda never been on.
This incident woulda lasted about
fifteen seconds.
The reason that we lost upper body control holds,
because we had something like
seventeen to twenty deaths, in a period of about 1975-76 to 1982.
And they said it was associated
with, it was being used on blacks,
and blacks were dying.
Now
the so-called community leaders
came forward and complained,
(He drinks water.)
and they started the hysteria
about the upper body control holds
that it was inhumane use of force.
And Gilbert Lindsay,
who was a really neat man,
when he saw a demonstration on the baton,
he made a statement
that "you're not gonna beat my people with the baton."
I want you to use the chokehold on 'em,
and a couple other people said
I don't care, you beat 'em into submission,
you break their bones,
you're not chokin' 'em anymore.
So the political framework was laid,
for eliminating upper body control holds
and Daryl Gates
I believe but I can't prove it
but his attitude supports it.
I started seeing a lot of incidents similar to Rodney King,
and some of them identical to Rodney King.
And I said, we gotta find some alternative uses of force.
And their attitude was:

"Don't worry about it,
don't worry about it."
And the last conversation I had was with my commander,
"We gotta explore some techniques and we gotta explore some
options
And his response to me
"Sergeant Duke
I'm tired of hearing this shit.
We're gonna beat people into submission
and we're gonna break bones
and he said the police commission and the city council took this
away from us.
Do you understand that
Sergeant Duke?"
And I said "Yes, sir."
And I never brought it up again.
And that to me,
tells me
this is an "in your face" to the City Council and to the Police
Commission.
And like I said
I can't prove this,
but I believe Daryl Gates,
and the Command staff were gonna do an "in your face" to the
City Council
and police commission saying,
you took upper body control hold away from us —
now we're really gonna show you what you're gonna get.

ANONYMOUS MAN
Juror in Simi Valley trial

Your Heads in Shame

A white man, very simply dressed, in his living room in Simi Valley. Tall. Getting dark outside. A lamp on a timer clicks on during the interview. He speaks quietly, carefully. Wearing glasses. Sitting in a comfortable armchair. Very soft spoken. Very careful, as he talks.

As soon as we went
into the courtroom with the verdicts
there were plain
clothes policemen everywhere
you know I knew that
there would be people unhappy with the verdict
but I didn't expect near
what happened.
If I had known
what was going to happen
I mean it's not
it's not fair to say I would have voted a different
way
I wouldn't have,
that's not our justice system,
but I would have written a note to the judge saying
"I can't do this"
because of
what it put my family through.
Excuse me.
(Crying.)
So anyway
we started going out to the bus

and the police said
right away
"If there's rocks and bottles, don't worry
the glass on the bus is bulletproof."
And it's a sheriff bus they lock prisoners in.
There were some obnoxious reporters out there
and you know the police were trying to get us into the bus and
cover our faces
and
and this obnoxious reporter from *Channel 11 News* said
(His crying gets bigger here.)
"Why are you hiding your heads in shame? Do you know that
buildings are burning
and people are dying in South LA
because of you?"
(He stops crying.)
And watching on TV
and seeing all the political leaders,
Mayor Bradley,
and President Bush
condemning our verdicts.
I mean the jurors as a group we tossed around
was this a set up of some sort?
We just feel like we were pawns that were thrown away by the system.
I mean
the judge,
most of the jurors,
feel like when he was reading the verdicts,
he,
we thought we could sense a look of disdain on his face.
And he also said
Beforehand,
that after the verdicts came out,
He would like to come up and talk to us.
But after he got the verdicts,
he sent someone up and said he really didn't want to
do that then.
He had the right and power to

withhold our names for a period of time,
and he did not do that
he released them right away.
A lot of newspapers published our addresses.
The New York Times published the value of our homes.
We received threatening phone calls and letters.
We didn't answer the phone,
because it was just every three minutes.
One of the most disturbing things and a lot of the jurors
said that
the thing that bothered them that they received in the mail
more
than anything else
more than the threats was a letter from the KKK
saying ...
"We support you and if you need our help, if you want to join
our organization
we'd welcome you into our fold."
And we all just were
No oh!
God!

ROCKED

Whereas most of the rest of the play is played barefoot, this segment should be played in combat boots. This part of the play should look like a human riot. However the stage is when "Rocked" begins, it should be completely disheveled by the end. Video images of the school riot should be shown, if possible, between pieces. The transitions between piece to piece however, should be rapid. Whether one, two or twelve people perform this segment, there should be the feeling that the performers never finish any one segment. As a new segment begins it should be as if it is interrupting the segment before. Sound and music can be used to build the energy and pacing to its crescendo, which is Keith Watson's piece "Rage." If the design is that one person should do this section (even if several actors play the rest of the play), this must look like a tour de force, costumes flying as they are changed, direct, intentional movement from place to place.

JOE VIOLA
Television Writer

Butta-Boom

A white man, in his late forties, early fifties, glasses up on his forehead. In a sunny room in Los Angeles. Serving cheese and crackers to the interviewer. Very big, loud resonant voice. Excited. A "call" that announces the energy to come in this section.

For the first time
in my entire life,

my entire life,
I was terrified!
I was standing there,
Just-having-mailed-my-daughter's-registration-to-Berkeley, what better stroke!
And I was standing there when the first cars rolled by and this was like one-thirty in the afternoon,
and they … I saw a kid with a nine!
And he brought it up,
he didn't aim it directly at me but he said,
"I'm goin' to kill you, you motherfucker!"
or "You're dead, motherfucker."
Something like that.
Right here, right on the corner.
I-sat-back-down-like-my-ass-was-filled-with-cement,
Right on the corner!
Right here! "Butta boom!"

KEITH WATSON
Former Security Guard, Co-Assailant of Reginald Denny

A Movie

African American, twenties. In a hat suitable to the time.
Walking the full distance of the stage — owning the stage.
Loud. Announcing.

It was like
the end of the world!
It was like a whole other time!
It was a major disaster!
Man made!
A catastrophe!
You know what I mean?
That was a devastation!
I mean
the violence,
the destruction,
the terror?
I mean
that's something!
I mean I haven't seen a movie like that!
(Laughs.)

STANLEY K. SHEINBAUM
Former President, Los Angeles Police Commission

Hammer

Bow tie. Jacket. Stage Center.

When I heard about the verdict
which was not until about five-thirty,
I immediately headed downtown to Parker Center.
As I was driving down the Santa Monica Freeway,
I had one interesting mini-experience,
that told me there was going to be trouble.
Very simple thing.
There was a,
uh,
nice-black-recent-BMW,
small car,
in good shape,
and there was an Afro-ican, [sic]
uh,
African-American woman
driving it.
And a *man*
next to her,
also African-American,
and she ...
Her window was open.
As she was driving,
she had a *hammer* in her hand,
Waving it back and forth!
Out-the-window!
As she was driving!
And this was a very dramatic thing,

in a minor way
and it said to me:
Trouble!
As-I-pulled-into-the-garage-at-Parker-Center,
and it's now close to
six-thirty —
There's Daryl Gates *(Slowly.)*
getting into his car!
And I ask him,
"Where you goin'?"
"I got something I gotta do."
That was the only answer I got.
As you may have heard,
turned out that he was on his way to a *fund raiser*
right up here in Brentwood.
In the meantime,
after he heads out,
I get through with that,
wondering what the hell
was going on with *him!*
He's the *chief* and *this thing*
very well
may be falling apart!

SHELBY COFFEY III
Editor, Los Angeles Times

Big and Dreadful Things

Patrician, white, elegant, elite class. 40s or 50s, well-heeled. In his office on a stool or chair, with a coffee table in front of him, with a sizeable piece of cement, from a broken sidewalk. It looks like a sculpture. Pin-striped jacket, tie, good enunciation. Very very subtle Southern aspect to his voice, but aristocratic. Perfect diction, careful speech. Clear volume. Must hear every single word as clear and separate.

I've tried to maintain that in talking to people about the riots
that you had a vast even Shakespearean range of motives.
And I remember around somewhere,
between eight,
and uh nine o'clock,
we began to uhm
get uh uh
some *rocks* hitting the windows
on the third floor.
So
I went downstairs
uh uh with a couple of copy messengers.
I grabbed a pair of scissors *(Deliberate, slow.)*
A guy looked like he was coming in,
I shouted *(The "t" in shouted is enunciated.)* at him
with the scissors
and copy,
couple of copy, messengers with me.
My *wife* is an emergency room doctor,
and she said
because she feels she's considerably more in *tune*

with the type of people who go around with scissors,
and other weapons
(Pause.)
She said uh
why don't you just go upstairs,
and work with the copy?
Because you might not *(Slow, one word at a time.)*
do very well with the crowd you seem to want to be running
with.
but I wasn't
uh about to be stopped
Because there was a clear sense of
clearly big
and dreadful things
were happening.

KEITH WATSON
Former Security Guard, Co-Assailant of Reginald Denny

Rocked

Crossing the full length or width of the stage.

'Cause
what took place here?
Southern California was *rocked*.
You know?
I mean the the
the whole infrastructure
the foundation was *cracked*
Know what I'm sayin'?
The seams of that fine fabric,
that that Los Angeles image that we have?
That California? That sunshine?
You know?
See we showed the insides.
The core.
Follow what I'm saying?
That which is usually bypassed
or overlooked?
It came forward.
It
let it be *known*.

KATIE MILLER
Bookkeeper and Accountant

Pep Boys

A very large woman. African American. In an armchair. Wearing a baseball cap. A large, resonant, loud voice, fast speech. Repetitions of words, where indicated, is very important for the rhythm of this. This woman's presence is comparable to that of the large, full-voiced black woman gospel singer who "stops" shows.

I think this thing
about the Koreans and the blacks.
That wasn't altogether true
and I think that the Korean stores
that got burned in the black neighborhood that were Korean owned
it was due to lack of lack of
gettin' to know
the people that come to your store
That's what that was.
Now!
They talk about the looting looting
in Korea town.
Those wasn't blacks!
Those wasn't blacks!
Those was Mexicans!
In the Korean town!
We wasn't over there lootin' over there
lootin' over there!
But here,
in in this right here,
the stores that got looted for this one one reason,
only, is that know who you goin', know who

Just *know* people comin' to your store, that's all,
Just *respect* people comin' in there.
Give 'em their money,
stead of just "Give me your money and get out of my face!"
And it was the same thing with the sixty-five riots
same thing!
And this, they kept making a big
the blacks and the Koreans!
I didn't see that!
And now see like
Pep
Boys that right there.
I didn't like the idea of Pep Boys myself.
I didn't like the idea of them hittin' Pep
Boys.
Only reason I can think they hit 'em is they too damn high!
That's the only reason, other than that!
I think that Pep Boys just
Came, people say
To hell with Pep boys Miney Mo and Jack!
Let me just go in here
I'm get me some damn
whatever the hell they have in there!"
Now I didn't loot this time.
Get that out!
Because in my mind, it's more
than that
you know.
But I didn't loot this time.
I was praising the ones that had
you know.
"You oughta burn that sucker down!" *(Very loud, yelling.)*
But after it was over
we went touring
call it touring,
all around.
And we went to that Magnin store.
Seein' people comin' out of that Magnin store.

And I was so
damn-mad-at-that-Paul-Moyer.
He's a damn newscaster.
He was on Channel 7.
Now that sucker's on Channel 4.
Makin' eight million dollars!
What the hell?
Person can make eight million dollars for readin' a piece of paper!
But that's a different story!
Highest in any newscaster!
I don't know why
to read some damn paper! *(Very loud.)*
I don't give a damn who tells me the damn news
long as they can *talk!*
Long as I can understand 'em!
I don't care
but that's a different story!

OCTAVIO SANDOVAL
Occupation Unknown

Bunk Beds

In a cowboy hat. A fifteen year old from Central America.
Heavy accent. Big smile. Nervous, shy, about the interview.
Not certain he wants to give the interview. "Camera shy." In
his living room, with friends around, teasing him in Spanish
and looking on. Sitting on a table.

For us to go in there looting.
I said I'll go in there and help you out then.
It was the second day
when everything had started.
And the first day we was just like out cruisin' around,
lookin' at the things bein' looted and stuff.
And the second day that's when we were right here
and he said
Let's go across the street and see what we can get.
You know like the cops wasn't,
doing nothing.
So we said,
Oh I guess it's okay.
So we went,
we went across the street.
That's where we got the beds from
and we just got like two beds and then we got them here.
They were bunk beds.
They were bunk beds.
And my neighbors, I guess,
went and told on me.
And my Dad, he was the one that,
And my Mom

they didn't really want the beds here.
So
They,
I was gone,
I was out that day,
and when I came back they wasn't here no more.
They just told me they took 'em to a church we used to go before.

FEDERICO SANDOVAL
Octavio's Brother

Channel 2, 4 ...

Bigger, older, confident. Glad to talk. Deep voice. In charge.
The author had gone to interview Octavio and there is a
sense that Federico took over: the alpha. Sitting on a surface
other than a chair. The words "for example" are key.

We didn't really even started,
not even to notice about each other.
Until a couple of weeks after.
For example, we were interested in what was going on.
You know, for example, the Rodney King incident.
But it didn't happen at that present moment.
A lot of people didn't know what was going on.
Many people were just there.
'Cause other people were there.
That was it.
They didn't know why.
I'm pretty sure most of the Hispanics didn't even know why.
'Cause basically the Rodney King basically came out,
on channel two, four, five, seven, nine, eleven, and thirteen.
Basically, no Hispanic news people really came out with it.
Not until after the incidents.
Not until after the riots started.
Basically a lot of Hispanics didn't even know.

KATIE MILLER
Bookkeeper and accountant

I. Magnin

Walking over to her chair, slowly, it is effortful, finally sitting somewhere, mid-speech.

Anyway we went to Magnin
and we seen people run in there and looted.
It's on Wilshire.
Very exclusive store.
For very, you know,
you have to have money to go in there to buy something.
And the people I seen runnin' out there that didn't have money to buy.
And I turned on the TV,
and here is Mr. Paul Moyer,
saying
"Yeah
they they uh
some people looted uh
I. Magnin,
I remember goin' to that store when I was a child.
What he call 'em?
He called 'em *thugs!*
These thugs goin' into that store!
I say "Hell with you *asshole!*"
That was my my,
I say "Okay! Okay!" for them to run into these *other* stores
You know?
"But don't go in no store,
that I I grew up on that has,
that my parents

took me to,
that is
expensive!
These stores
they ain't supposed to be to be
looted!
How dare you loot a store
that rich people go to!
I mean the nerve of them!" *(Slight pause.)*
I-found-that-very-offensive!
Who the hell does he think he is?
Oh, but that was another story!
They lootin' over here,
but soon they loot this store he went to
Oh he was all pissed!
It just made me sick!
But that's another story too!

TALENT AGENT
Anonymous Hollywood Agency

Caesar Salad

Easy, low voice, not to be overheard. In an office in an impeccably designed building. Fine furnishings in the office. Armani jacket, or comparable, fine tie. Friendly demeanor, almost as if telling a secret.

There was still the uneasiness that was growing.
When the fuse was still burning.
But
it was,
Business as usual!
Basically.
You got
such and so on line one,
such and so on line two,
traffic,
Wilshire,
Santa Monica.
Bunch of us hadda go to lunch at the
the Grill. *(Enunciated.)*
In Beverly Hills
um
'gain *(As in "again" without the a.)* major
show business dead center business restaurant.
Kinda *loud* but *genteel.*
The there was an insipient [sic] *panic.*
You could just *feel*
the tension.
In the *(Pronounced "thee.")*
restaurant

was palpable.
Was tangible.
You could cut it with a knife.
Everywhere,
is all anyone was talking,
about you could hear little bits
of information …
"Did ya hear?
Did ya hear?"
It's like we were transmitting
thoughts
to each other
all across the restaurant.
We were transmitting thoughts to each other.
All the
Frankly, the
white
upper class,
upper-middle-class
whatever your
the
definition is
white, successful,
spending too much money,
too ya know, too good a restaurant,
that kinda thing.
We were just,
getting ourselves into a *frenzy*
Which I think a lot of it,
involved,
guilt.
Just *generic-guilt.*
When we drove back,
and it's about ten-minute drive,
talking about the need *(singsong)*
for guns
to protect ourselves,
It had just gone from there to there!

But I'm tellin' you nothin' happened!
I don't mean somebody in the restaurant,
had a fight,
or somebody screamed at someone,
nothing just,
ya know,
"Caesar salad
da de da"
Ya know
but the whole
bit
went
like that! *(Slow, more intense, lower volume, but more direct, hunkering down to the audience.)*
We walked in
from the underground garage into here and we looked at each other,
and we could see people
running around!
Instead of like
people walk fast in this business,
but now they were they were like
running!
And
we looked at ourselves,
"We've gotta close the office!"
so we had gone from,
I'm a little nervous
to "We gotta close the office
shut down!"
This is a business
we don't shut down!

ELAINE YOUNG

Real Estate Agent from early scenes
The Beverly Hills Hotel

At her desk, with her glasses on.

So the second day,
I had a date.
And he lives about twenty minutes away in the Valley and they say,
"Don't drive freeways."
And I said, "Are you going to see me tonight?
'Cause I was just three weeks separated and I don't want to be alone."
And he said, "Yeah."
So he came to pick me up.
And he got there and I said, "Oh my God, where are we gonna *go?*
We can't eat *anywhere.* Everything is *closed.*"
And I said,
"*Wait* a minute! A *hotel* wouldn't be closed. *They* gotta be serving food."
So I said, "Let's see if we can go to the Beverly Hills Hotel."
And when I got there, much to my *shock,*
The-whole-town-picture-business-people,
had decided to do the same thing!
So basically, what happened the three or four days of the heavy rioting,
people were going to the hotel.
And I mean it was *mobbed.*
So we would stay there till three or four in the morning.
Everybody was talking
"What was going on?" *(Singsong.)*
And "How could this happen in California?"
And "Oh my God, what's happened to our town?"
And "These poor people ... " and, and, and totally down and down

and down.

So when they interviewed me with the closing of the Polo Lounge —

I went there thirty-six years for lunch.

I wrote my book there,

Well ... the book starts out: "As I drove my car to the Beverly Hills Hotel ... "

And during the riots

'Cause it was so foremost on my mind.

And I was talking about how we were all *there.*

Some *man* wrote me a letter.

"To Mrs. Young.

You are really an asshole.

You take life so lightly.

I saw your interview on television.

As far as I'm concerned,

you're a dumb shit bimbo,

talking about having fun during the riots at the Polo Lounge.

How stupid can you be.

You're an embarrassment." *(Seems shocked.)*

I mean, oh my God, I'm reading this letter.

I got it three weeks ago.

That's when the Polo Lounge closed.

It was like

Oh my God!

If he only left his number!

So I can call him and explain that in no way did I mean to be *flippant* on television about the riots.

It was like people hanging out together.

So then you say, "Well let me put this out of my mind for a while and go on"

like safety in numbers.

No one can hurt us at the Beverly Hills Hotel

'cause it was like a fortress!

So that was the mood at the Polo Lounge

"Here we are,

and we're still alive" —

and, you know,

"We hope there'll be people alive

when we come out!"
(If possible, the same actor playing Elaine Young should become Keith Watson and turn the desk over.)

KEITH WATSON
Former Security Guard, Co-Assailant of Reginald Denny

Rage

Having thrown over the desk of Elaine Young and walking the length of the stage in his hat, he now topples other things on the stage, in a full blown out expression of rage. This did not happen in reality — but is meant to use whatever stage language there is to try to embody the rage, power, pain, disappointment of black youth at the center of their identification of the riot with Rodney King. Pain and the glee that accompanied the frenzy of the riot are a part of the rage.

It was rage,
black rage,
that's what I like ta
call it,
you know what I mean?
Black-rage!
And then when I look at that video and see how upset,
the blacks were?
They were upset!
Extremely upset!
I look at I look at now since I been home!
I look at all the
vacant lots
they tore up a lot of stuff!
(He laughs.)
No wonder they were so upset hunh!
(Moving about the stage, threatening the audience perhaps.)
It was like a storm!
Like the eye of a storm!
You know, it was a whirlwind.

And I was in the eye of it?
Know what I'm saying?
Know how a tornado kicks up the winds like that?
(An earnest explanation.)
You got to realize the not guilty verdicts,
was *heavy* on everybody's mind
I followed the trial cause I wanted to see if justice works
and on that particular day justice didn't work.
Yes! I was upset.
I was *highly* upset!
That could've been *me* out there gettin' my ass whooped!
and these four officers could a walked away for whoopin' my ass
like that?
I'm-afraid-not
I wasn't raised to take ass whoopin's like that and turn the other
cheek
I refused!
*(He/She is just about to throw the cement rock on Shelby Coffey's desk
when he/she either becomes Shelby Coffey III, or the actor playing
Shelby Coffey III retrieves it (easily) from him/her and launches into
Coffey's piece.)*

SHELBY COFFEY III
Editor, Los Angeles Times

Beirut

Taking the rock, and sitting in the debris.

And rocks,
of which these are souvenirs,
were being tossed in.
And later on in the evening one person threw a makeshift Molotov
cocktail.
We got a *call* from our
uh *stringer* in *Bei-rut** wondering if we were alright
You-know-you've-got-some-trouble-in-your-city-when-your-
stringer
from *Bei-rut**
calls to say, "Are you,
are you *al-right*?"

* *Note: "r's" in "beirut" and "alright" are well pronounced.*

83

JUDITH TUR
Ground Reporter L.A. News Service

War Zone

Music. Stage is put back in order. Screen comes down, shows the beating of Reginald Denny, a white truck driver, by four young black men. (Available: L.A. News Service.)

A white woman in her fifties. Cowboy boots, nice shirt. She is facing the screen and talking the audience through the video.

Anna,
This is the beginning of the riots.
And, uh,
this is the video we're going to be giving you for the show.
Now watch this, Anna.
This is absolutely,
I think,
disgraceful.
Here's a gang member.
Here …
This is
a live broadcast, by the way.
These poor …
He fell like a sack of potatoes.
I mean, real brave men, right?
Now these women here —
you'll see them later —
are taking pictures of this.
This is sick.
So this is the video I'm gonna be …
that I'm gonna give you for the show.
I'm gonna fast-forward here,

because you can see him
getting up
and nobody's helping him.
These two men try to help
him.
"Football" *(Referring to Damian "Football" Williams, felt to be the
leader of the beating.)*
tells them something.
"Get away."
Okay?
Look at this
decrepit old man
and look at these,
these clowns
here.
Anybody with any kind
of a heart would go over and try and help.
Here's Reginald Denny passing by.
If you saw an animal being beaten, you would go over and help an
Animal.
Okay, here's a black man
going and helping.
I think his name is, um,
Larry
Tarvo.
T-a-r-v-o.
And this gentleman here is getting his glasses and trying to help
him
and …
He risked his life doing that.
Now you'll see Reginald Denny
and I look at this and each time I see this
I get angrier and angrier.
Because there was no reason for this to have happened.
Okay, here's another animal
videotaping this guy.
These people have no heart.
These people don't deserve

to live.
Sorry for getting emotional,
but I mean this is not my United States anymore.
This is sicko.
Did you see him shoot him?
Did you see that?
(Rewinds the tape.)
This is like being in a war zone.
This is the guy with the gun —
Pulls out the rifle —
You see
the shot?
He missed Reginald Denny!
He missed him!
But he doesn't even run across the street.

KEITH WATSON
Former Security Guard, Co-Assailant of Reginald Denny

Make My Mark

Sober, still, quiet. Facing audience straight on.

I mean,
you go through life
and you always want to
uh make a mark or leave a mark
to show that you passed
through this
through life
you understand what I'm saying?
Never *(Laughing.)*
in my wildest dreams,
did I think that,
something like this
would have happened in order for
me to make my mark,
leave my mark.
I mean I'm up there with Martin and Malcolm.
And to have my name uttered in the same breath as those two gen-
tlemen, I'm talkin' about Martin Luther King, and Malcolm X.
That's *heavy.*

DARYL GATES
Former Chief of Los Angeles Police Department

It's Awful Hard to Break Away

Standing simply, in front of stage. Simple cotton jacket.

First of all, I I don't think it was a fund raiser.
I don't think it was a fund raiser at all.
It was a group of
people
who were in opposition
to proposition F
We're talking about long-term support.
We're talking about people who
came out and supported me right from the beginning
of of this controversy.
When people were trying to get me to retire and everything else.
Real strong supporters
of of mine
And they *begged* me to be there.
And I said I would and this is before we knew the the
uh verdicts were coming in
and I didn't wanna go.
I didn't like those things I don't like them at all.
But
strong supporters, and I said "I'll drop by for a little while
I'll drop by."
And um so I had a commitment.
And I'm a person who tries very hard to keep commitments.
And somewhere along the way,
better sense
should have
prevailed

not because it would have changed
the course of of events in any way shape or form it wouldn't have.
When I when I thought when things were getting
to the point that I had we were having some serious problems,
I was almost there.
My driver said "We're almost there Chief, we're almost there."
My intent was to drop in say "Hey
I think we got a a uh
riot blossoming
I can't stay I gotta get out of here"
and that's basically what I did.
My intent was
to say hey I I gotta get outta here say hi
and that's what I intended to do
and it's awful hard ta
break away
I kept walking toward the door, walking toward the door
people want a picture
shake your hands
and it took longer than I thought.

TALENT AGENT
Anonymous Hollywood Agency

Absorb a Little Guilt

Recurrence of talent agent, same set up, office chair, jacket, tie

Memo goes
out saying
office closed for the day
Everyone please leave
the office and then
I remember somebody said
"Did you *hear* they're burning down
the Beverly Center!"
By the way "They"
No, no, No it's
there is no "who"
"Whaddya mean *who*
No just they that's fair enuf
Did you hear *they* are burning down the Beverly Center!
Oh, okay "they"
ya know, what I mean?
It almost didn't matter *who*
it's irrelevant
"*somebody*
It's not *us!*"
That was one of the highlights for me
So I'm looking outside,
and the traffic is *far* worse.
And people were basically *fleeing* the office.
And we were closing all the blinds,
and this is about
um

I guess by about four o'clock.
Thee [sic] vision of all these yuppies
and aging, of aged *yuppies*
Armani suits,
And you know
fleeing like
wild-eyed
All you needed was *Godzilla* behind them
You know
like this *(He gestures as Godzilla.)*
chasing them out of the building!
That's really it
Aaah aaah!
(He laughs.)
Still
Still,
nothing had happened
I don't mean to tell you that *bombs* were exploding.
Nothing Zero!
So we
I was one of the last to leave,
as usual.
And the roads were so *packed,* it
it must be like
they were leaving
Hiroshima
or something
Dresden …
I've never been in a war or
Just the daily-war-of
(Intercom beeps.)
Who's that? *(Sudden, very alert, like a mother alert to her baby's cry,
jumping up, leaving and coming back.)*
Do you need me?
One sec …
Where was I?
Yeah,
What what was,

Was I deserve it
You know
Was I was I getting
my
when I was *fearing*
for
safety
or my family or something
those moments
because the panic was so *high*
(Where's the nanny?
Where's the kids?)
That, oh my God!
I was almost thinking
"Did I deserve this?"
"Do I do I deserve it?"
I thought me personally, uh, *no*
generically,
maybe *so*
Even though, I I
what's *provoked* it
it was
the spark
was the verdict
which was
ab-surd!
But that was just the *spark.*
This had been set
for years before.
But maybe,
not maybe,
but uh the
system
plays unequally
and the people who were
the "they,"
who were burning down the Beverly Center,
had been victims of the system

whether well intentioned or not.
Somebody got the short shift
and *they* did
and I started to
absorb a little guilt,
and say uh
I deserve
I deserve it.
I don't mean I deserve to get my house *burned down*
The *us*
did
not in
not
I like to think not *intentionally*
but
maybe so
There's just
It,
's so
awful out there
it was so *heart*breaking
seeing those
the *devastation* that went on
and people reduced to *burning down their own neighborhoods*
burning down our neighborhoods
I could see
But burning down their *own*
that was more dramatic
to me.

ELVIRA EVERS
General Worker and Cashier, Canteen Corporation

To Look Like Girls from Little

With a baby bottle in her hand. At her kitchen table. A black woman from Panama in her forties. Children can be heard O.S. A Panamanian accent. She had a gold front tooth.

So,
it was like a carnival out there
and I say
to my friend Frances
"Frances, you see this?"
and she said, "Girl, you should see
that
is getting worse."
And I say, "Girl, let me take my butt
up there before something happen."
and um
when somebody throw a bottle
and I just,
then I felt,
like moist
and it was like a tingling sensation right?
And I dida like this *(Touching her stomach.)*
and it was like itchin',
and I say, "Frances, I'm *bleedin'.*"
And she walk with me to her house
And she say, "Lift up your gown, let me see."
She say, "Elvira, iss a bullet!"
I say, "What?"
I say, "I didn't heard nothin'."
She say, "Yes, but iss a bullet."

She say, "Lay down there. Let me call St. Francis and tell them that
you been shot
and to send a ambulance."
and she say,
"Why you,
you don't mess with none of those people
Why they have to shoot you?"
So Frances say the ambulance be here in fifteen minutes
I say, "Frances,
I cannot wait that."
I say,
"I'm goin'!"
So I told my oldest son I say,
"Amant take care your brothers
I be right back."
Well by this time he was standing there he was crying.
All of them was crying.
What I did for them not to see the blood,
I took the gown and I cover it,
and I didn't cry
that way they didn't get nervous.
And I get in the car
I was goin' drive
Frances say, "What you doin'?"
I said, "I'm drivin'."
She say, "No, you're not!"
And we take all the back street,
and she was so supportive
because she say, "You alright?
You feel cold?
You feel dizzy?
The baby move?"
she say, "You nervous?"
I say, "No, I'm not nervous, I'm just worried about the baby."
I say, "I don't want to lose this baby."
She say, "Elvira everything will be alright." She say, "Just pray."
So there was a lot of cars we had to be blowing the horn
So finally we get to St. Francis *(Hospital.)*

95

and Francis told the front desk office she say,
"She been shot!"
and they say, "What she doin' walkin'?"
and I say, "I feel alright."
Everybody stop doin' what they was doin'
and they took me to the room
and put the monitor to see if the baby was fine
and they find the baby heart beat
and as long as I heard the baby heart beat I calmed down.
Long as I knew whoever it is boy or girl, it's alright,
and
matter of fact my doctor, Doctor Thomas, he was there
at
the emergency room
what a coincidence, right?
I was just lookin' for that familiar face
and soon as I saw him
I say, "Well I'm alright now."
Right?
So he bring me this other doctor and then told me:
"Elvira, we don't know how deep is the bullet
we don't' know where it went. We gonna operate on
you.
But since that we gonna operate we gonna take the baby out
and you don't have to
go through all of that."
They say, "Do you understand
what we're saying?"
I say, "Yeah!"
and they say, "Okay sign here."
And I remember them preparing me
and I don't remember anything else
Nella! *(Calling to her child.)*
No.
(Turns to the side and admonishes the child, a girl about five years old.)
She likes company.
And in the background
I remember Dr. Thomas say you have a six-pound-twelve-ounces

little girl
he told me how much she weigh and her length
and he
say, "Um
she born
she had the bullet in her elbow,
but when we remove,
when we clean her up,
we find out that the bullet was still between two joints
so we did operate on her and your daughter is fine
and you are fine."
(Sound of a little child saying "Mommy.")
Nella!
She *wants to show the baby.*
(Listening to a question.)
Jessica. *(Is her name.)*
Bring the baby, Nella *(The baby is brought [imaginary]. She laughs.)*
Yes — *(Listening to a question.)*
yes
We don't like to keep the girls without earrings, we like the little girls
to look like girls from little.
I pierce hers
when I get out on Monday
by Wednesday I did it.
So by Monday she was five days
she was seven days,
and I
pierced her ears.
And the red band is just like for evil eyes
we really believe in Panama ...
In English I can't explain too well.
And her doctor he told,
he explain to me,
that the bullet
destroyed the placenta
and
went through me
and she caught in her arm.

(Here you can hear the baby making noise, and a bell rings.)
If she didn't caught it in her arm,
Me, and her, would be dead.
See,
So it's like
open your eyes!
Watch what is goin' on!

JESSYE NORMAN
Opera Singer

Roar

*Large, beautiful. On an English ottoman, sipping tea. There is
a lot of musicality in her very resonant voice — lots of variety
of pitches. By the end, she is at a very low, deep tone.*

I mean it's all confusion
and the more we talk about this
the more facets of this confusion I can understand and see.
I was coming back from having
given a performance in Seattle,
so I was in Los Angeles
on the day of the riot.
And some friends of mine,
who are very involved
in in
things
having to do with civil rights,
said "You know
you ought to stay"
I said
"I can't" *(She says the word "can't" like no one I've heard before, as if
she has to say it often.)*
I have to
you know, I'm in the middle of a tour,
"I *can't.*"
So
I was in the plane thinking:
"Well, gosh, I didn't have time to stay in Los Angeles
and what would I have done anyway
besides go to somebody's church and sing a few songs?

What could I have done?
except
to
talk or to sing
to somebody who would listen
to me,
I don't think people were in the mood
to *sing* at that time
(In response to a remark by the author.)
Of course, of course
in the civil rights movement
you'd sing *first*
and then you would organize whatever, you know, protest was happening
that week or day or whatever.
And you would sing at the end of it as well!
And you'd sing all through it!
Black people have a great tradition of singing.
I mean this is how the spiritual came into *being*
that in order to,
deal with this
unbelievable
situation
of being transported
from one's homeland
and being made a *slave* we had to *sing* ourselves through that!
We didn't sing ourselves out of it
we sang ourselves through it!
But I think, that if I were
a person
already, you know, a teenager,
sort of a youngster,
Twenty or something,
And I felt I were being *heard* for the first time
it would not be singing as we know it
It would be a *roar.*
(Slight pause.)
Oh I think it would be a roar

Oh it would come
oh it would come, from the bottom of my feet!
It would be
I really think that
it would be like a *lion*
just *roaring*
It wouldn't be singing, as we know it
It wouldn't be words
It would just be
like-the-earth's-first-utterance.
I really do feel so.

TWILIGHT: LOS ANGELES, 1992

ACT TWO

LOSSES

CORNEL WEST
Scholar

Chekhov/Coltrane

Wearing cufflinks, a black vest, tie, white shirt, no jacket, in an easy chair with table and lamp (the interview took place in a hotel room). Sipping cognac from a snifter and at some point lighting a long, brown cigarette. This piece is a verbal tour de force, and must be spoken with swiftness and passion, and the actor must completely understand its complexity, speaking it as if it were everyday, simple speech.

To use the language of decline
decay and despair
Rather than doom gloom and
no possibility
Because I think any talk about
despair is not where you end but
where you start
and *then* the courage and the sacrifice
come in
and *at the level of hope*
not optimism.
Hope and optimism are different.
Optimism tends to be based on
the notion that there's enough
evidence out there that
allows us to think things are going
to be better
much more rational

deeply secular
(No breaths in the following fifteen lines: nonstop.)
whereas *hope*
looks at the evidence and says
it doesn't look good at *all!*
and says
it doesn't look good at all
We gonna make a leap of
faith *beyond* the evidence
to attempt to create
new possibilities based
on visions that
become contagious so
people can engage in heroic
actions always
against the odds, no guarantee whatso*ever*.
That's hope!
I'm a prisoner of hope though.
I'm on die a prisoner of hope.
I never believe
misery and despair have the last word,
(You were asking about the loss in black life)
For black folks our loss
is the loss of the feeling that we
can be *whole*
in a society that spends so much
time de-human-izing us
The sheer *joy* of being human
has been truncated
We've created certain spaces
where we can take off the mask
and be ourselves.
Our churches,
our nightclubs,
certain streets,
but they are very circumscribed, and
in the end they are still haunted,
by the ghosts of white supremacy.

(Even as they are acts of liminality,
letting it all hang out)
So what happens is you have a very very uh,
I think,
Indescribable,
one of the reasons I spend a lot of time
with *Chekhov*
and *Tolstoy,*
he's much more *nihilistic* than Doestoyevsky
and what I love about Tolstoy
and the *great* Chekhov,
Brother Anton,
the greatest artist of the twentieth century—
He only had a few plays up
to 1904
and then he's gone
starts 1900,
and like black folk he's able to get
at the depths of a level of,
sadness and sorrow,
and boredom and horror,
and agony and anguish,
and stay there!
And not still end up with despair!
He's still compassionate!
He empathizes at such a deep level!
But the reason why he's comic,
rather than tragic
is that he *allows* himself to linger longer
on the different manifestations
of sadness and sorrow.
He doesn't skip over!
You were suggesting that the Negro spiritual
is an adequate expression of our loss,
our problem has been that
either we accept a certain
Christian eschatology
that wants to get to Easter too soon!

Doesn't want to stay either on the cross
or on Saturday when God is dead!
That's what black folk are *Saturday* people!
Catholic Church puts on purple
All over the church
No sense that Easter is coming really. It's deep
You know Paul, says in Romans Eight
"The creation groaneth and travaileth
in fu-til-ity!"
You talkin' about Saturday!
That's a Saturday situation that's
us!
Saturday people!
Now Richard Pryor:
The Pryor comes close.
Oh! Oh! My God.
He's talkin' about
forms of sadness not just sadness
but *melancholia*
Shot through with black rage!
Cause black rage is a
component of our black condition,
see.
But if whites experienced black sadness ... *(Pause.)*
It would be too overwhelming for them. *(Pause.)*
Very few white people could
actually take seriously,
black sadness and live the lives that
they livin:
livin' in denial
"Oh it couldn't be that bad"
And they have their own form of sadness
Tends to be linked to
the American Dream
But it's a very very very different kind of
Sadness.
And don't get me wrong,
I think that

Melville, Faulkner, Thomas Pynchon,
Mark Twain,
Dreiser.
There have been great, so-called white
American artists,
all getting at what I'm getting at —
Dreiser,
and Twain is shot through!
Now
Toni,
who I think is the greatest
so-called black writers,
Toni gets at it more
than any of the *novelists*
But
Coltrane
understood it.
To have that level of empathy and
sensitivity
in a,
not morally dead
but morally tone-deaf society,
tremendous creativity,
Coltrane!
It was thanks to Miles [Davis] and
others who loved him enough
to allow him to
express himself.
103rd Street Rhythm Band!
Used to put it
"Let the brother express himself,
he got some things to get out!
You know
Ask Miles
"How come you let Coltrane play
for an hour and ten minutes?"
"That's how long it takes him to say what
he has to say!"

"Miles only played for twelve minutes."
Miles said
"Let him take his time"
Let the brother blow say what he got
   to say!"
'Magine what our black leaders would
do
Get off the stage let me start up!
My turn
Or academics — My turn.
But Miles said … "Got to let him get the stuff out … "

REGINALD DENNY
Semi-Truck Driver, Victim

A Weird Common Threat in Our Lives

In a bright orange or yellow jacket and baseball cap. In his lawyer (Johnnie Cochran)'s office. Holding a large daytime organizer and a ring of keys.

I knew something was wrong when they bashed in the
right window of
my truck!
That's the end of what I remember as far as anything
until five or six days later.
They say it was in a coma,
Morphine is what they were givin' me for pain.
and it was just an interesting time
I think when it really dawned on me,
that something big might had happened,
was when very important people wanted to come in and say hi.
The person that I remember that wanted to come in and see me,
the first person that I was even aware of who wanted to see me,
was Reverend Jesse Jackson
and I'm just thinkin':
"Not this guy!
that's the dude I see on TV all the time!"
And then it was a couple days later that
Arsenio Hall *(Stretching out "Hall.")* came to see me.
And then, about then, I started to uh
started to get it.
And by the time I left Daniel Freeman Hospital, I knew what happened,
except they wouldn't let me watch it on TV.
I mean they completely controlled that remote control thing

they just had it on a movie station.
And talking to Titus and Bobby and Terry and Lee
that's the four people
who came to my rescue.
You know, they're telling me stuff that I would never
even have known!
Terry,
I met only because she came as a surprise-guest-visit-to-the-hospital.
That was an emotional time. *(Pause.)*
How does one say that,
someone
saved
my life?
How does a person
how do *I*
express-enough-
thanks
for someone risking their
neck, for *me*
And then I was kind of
I don't know if "afraid" is the word
I was just a little,
felt a little awkward meeting people
who
saved me.
Meeting them was not like meeting
a stranger
but it was like,
meeting a
buddy!
There was a *weird* common thread in our lives.
And here is four people —
who seen it on TV
and said "Enough's enough!"
and came to my rescue.
They tell me
I drove the truck for what, about a hundred or so feet.
And it's been seventeen years since I got outta high school.

I been driving semis since then.
It's almost second nature,
(it doesn't take much brains to do it)
The doctors say there's a *fight* or *flight* syndrome.
And I guess I was in *flight!*
But Bobbi
Green
saw that I was getting nowhere fast and he just jumped in and scooted me over
and drove the truck.
By this time
it was tons of glass and blood everywhere
'cause I've seen pictures of what I looked like
when I first went into surgery
and I mean it was a pretty
bloody mess.
And they showed me my hair,
when they cut off my hair
they gave it to me in a plastic bag?
And it was just
long hair and
glass and blood.
Lee
that's a woman
Lee Euell
she told me
she just
cradled me
There's no
passenger seat in the truck
and here I am, just kind of on my knees in the middle of the floor
and uh,
Lee's just covered with blood
and Titus is on one side
'cause Bobby couldn't see out the window
the front windshield was so badly broken
it was hard to see
and Titus is standing on the running board telling Bobbi where to

go
and then Terri
Titus's girlfriend,
She's in *front* of the truck, weaving through traffic,
dodging *towards* cars
to get them ta
kind of move out of the way,
to get them to clear a path,
and next stop was
Daniel-Freeman-Hospital!
Someday, when I
uh
get a house
I'm gonna have one of those *rooms*
and it's just gonna be
of all the riot stuff
and it won't be a
blood and guts
memorial
It's not gonna be a sad
it's gonna be a happy room
it's gonna be
of all the crazy things that I've got
all the
the
love and compassion
and the funny notes
and the letters from far away places
just framed, placed
framed things
Where a person will walk in,
and just have a good old time in there!
It'll just be
fun to be in there,
just like a fun thing.
And there won't be
a color problem
in this room.

You take the toughest
white guy
who thinks he's a bad ass
and
thinks he's better than any other race in town,
Get him in a position where he needs help,
he'll take the help.
From no matter who the color of the guy across,
because he's so self-
centered and serving,
he'll take it.
And then
soon as he's better,
he'll turn around
and rag on 'em
(Pause and intense stare, low key, then listening to a question from the author.)
What?
I don't know what I want.
I just want people to wake up
It's not a color it's a person!
So this room,
it's just gonna be
people
just a wild place!
It's gonna be a blast.
One day, it'll happen.
Lord
willing it'll happen.

PAUL PARKER
Chairperson, Free the L.A. Four Plus Defense Committee*

No Justice, No Peace/My Room

*A well-built black man in his twenties, with a pencil, legal
pad, and wearing African garb, speaks rapidly.*

They accused my brother Lance
of attempted murder,
of shootin' at Reginald Denny,
um, with a shotgun.
They said he attempted to blow up some gas pumps.
And my father got shot in the streets eleven years ago
over a petty robbery,
and their attitude was "We don't want to bring your family
through the trauma and drama, just stir
up some trouble."
They basically feel that if it's a nigger killin' a nigger,
a black on black crime,
they don't have no problem with that.
But let it be a white victim?
Oh, they gonna … they gonna go,
to any extremes necessary
to basically convict some black people.
Denny is white, Denny is white,
that's the bottom line.
If Denny was Latino,
Indian, or black,
they wouldn't give a damn,
they would not give a *damn*.
Because many people got beat,

* *The "L.A. Four" were four black men on trial for beating Reginald Denny.*

116

but you didn't hear about the Lopezes or the Vaccas
or the, uh, Quintanas
or the, uh,
Tarvins.
You didn't hear about them,
but you heard about the Reginald Denny beating,
the Reginald Denny beating,
the Reginald Denny beating.
This one white boy
paraded all around
this nation
to go do every talk show there is,
get paid left and right.
Oh, Reginald Denny,
this innocent white man.
"Innocent?"
I don't see it on the innocent tip,
because if that's the case,
then we supposed to have some empathy
or some sympathy toward this one white man?
It's like well, how 'bout the empathy and the sympathy toward *blacks?*
You know, like I said before, we innocent. Like I said,
you *kidnapped* us,
you raped our women,
you pull us over daily,
have us get out of our cars,
sit down on the curb,
you go through our cars,
take all our papers out,
go through our trunk,
and drive off,
don't even give us a ticket!
You know, *we* innocent,
You know
where's *our* justice?
Where's *our* self-respect?
But, hey, you want us to feel something toward
this *white* man, this *white* boy.

I'm like *please,*
It ain't happenin' here, not from the real brothers and sisters?!
That white man ...
some feel that white boy just better be glad he's alive.
'Cause a lot of us didn't make it.
They caught it on video,
Some brothers beatin' the shit out of a white man,
And they did everything in they power-to-convict-these-brothuhs.
"No-Justice, No-Peace."
That's just more or less, I guess you could say, my motto.
It basically just means if there's no justice here
then we not gonna give them any peace.
Peace of body. Peace of mind.
You might have a dent ... a dent in your head from now on in life.
It might not be you —
but it may be your daughter!
You know somewhere in your family you won't have no peace.
(Pause.)
When I finally get my house, I'm gonna have just one room, set aside.
It's gonna be my "No Justice No Peace" room.
Gonna have up on the wall "No Justice,"
over here "No Peace,"
and have all my articles,
and clippings and, um,
everything else.
I guess so my son can see,
my children can know what Daddy did.
You know, if I still happen to be here,
God willin',
they can just see what it takes
to be a strong black man,
what you gotta do for your people,
you know.
When God calls you, this is what you gotta do.
You either stand or you fall.
You either be black or you die.
(Pause.)

We didn't get to Beverly Hills but
that doesn't mean we won't get there
You keep it up!
um
They're talkin' about "You burned down your own neighbor-
hoods."
And I say, "First of all,
we burned down these *Koreans* in this neighborhood."
About ninety-eight percent of the stores that got burned down
were
Korean.
The Koreans was like the Jews in the day.
And we put them in check.

WALTER PARK
Store Owner, Gunshot victim

Kinda Lonely

A Korean-American man in his early sixties. He has been shot in the temple — so his speech is strained, he is blind in one eye from the wound. His body is intact, but he was basically lobotomized by the gunshot. Heavy accent. Deep, resonant vocal tones. He is groping for meaning. Birds, lawn mower in distance. A beautiful, light, airy living room with high ceilings and European art.

I felt kind of
Lonely.
You know
in the store.
So I said,
well
I might need go
travel somewhere
y'know.
And I said,
well I'm gonna probably go see
my Mom,
or you know,
somebody.
So I try to go to Korea.
Then I call a couple guys up
and
they uh,
I feel kinda lonely.
I wanna go Korea.
See if I can change uh

situation
and they didn't say nothing.
(Very passionate, and amazed. Birds and lawn mower closer.)
It's
kinda you know,
wondering thing.
And one guy happened to tell me,
"Why you wanna go Korea
for?
You just came out of
Hospital."
You know?
That
that makes me wonder too.
So, I came home and
I told my wife about it.
And she didn't say nothing.
It happens to
(His voice is much fuller here.)
among the Koreans,
among Orientals,
if they really *love* somebody or they really *like* somebody
they try
hide certain things.
For different manner.
And uh
I accepted it as different manner.
That
that's the way she loves
me, and it's fine
as long as I know,
and I have way to pay her back.
That makes it even.
And she didn't say nothing.

CHRIS OH
Medical Student, Stepson to Walter Park,
Son to Mrs. June Park

How Things Used to Be

Korean American. Early thirties, late twenties. California, or neutral accent. Deep resonant voice. Soft voice, swift speech. Not speaking English as a second language. Less weight than in the speech of Mr. and Mrs. Park. Not emotional. More informative, scientific. Direct.

Besides, you know, being his son
I also said "I'm a medical student
and
I'd like to know
what the prognosis is
and I'd like to know
what you've done."
And um
They didn't tell me anything.
And so here you are
and he's in this condition,
you don't know what he's already had
a bi frontal
partial lobectomy.
(Slight pause, responding to a question.)
Well, the bullet
passed through his temple,
temple side here,
and it went through his left eye,
and lodged,
in his frontal lobe.
It's

In the past
in the old days
they did a lot of frontal lobectomies,
when they just removed,
that part of the brain for people who are very tense and ...
Yeah,
lobotomies
and um,
the frontal lobe is
That's where your higher learning skills are,
your willingness to do things,
and your um,
I guess your basic character.
You know what when you have, when you think, and remember
how things used to be,
and you realize you can't do those things now,
you
look different,
and
you can't drive.
I know he wants to drive.
(He smiles.)

MRS. JUNE PARK
Wife of Walter Park

And in My Heart for Him

Pretty woman, in her fifties, very well taken care of. Impeccably, stylishly dressed. European designer suit and shoes. Jewelry. Hair, impeccably done. Groomed, manicured. Heavy accent. A sense when she and Chris Oh talk that Walter Park cannot understand them.

He came to United States
twenty-eight years
ago.
He was very high educated,
and also very nice person to the people.
And he has business about seven,
(Responding to correction.)
What? Ten years.
(Responding to correction.)
Twenty years.
So he work very hard.
And he *so* hard
And he also,
donated a lot of money to the Compton area,
and he knows the City Council
the policemen they knows him.
Then why
Why, he had to get shot?
(She cries.)
You know?
I don't know why
So really angry you know
Then I cry

most of my life.
This is the time I cry lot.
So
I go to the hospital and I stay with him
especially ICU room,
is they don't allow to the family
stay there.
But the,
all the nurses know me.
And every time I go there, I bring some nice donuts
to the nurses and doctors
and they find out how much I love him.
So they just let me in,
and stay with him all day long.
So I just feed him,
and stayed 'til eight o'clock,
at the night
and all day long
and I spend all my time
and in my heart for him.

CHRIS OH
Medical Student, Stepson of Walter Park

Execution Style

*Direct, factual, swift, clear, not emotional Of the three speakers,
his is the most direct address to the audience — almost as the
narrator for his parents. Variety in vocal pitch, melodic.*

When
he got shot,
I guess he
pressed on the accelerator
and he ran into a telephone pole.
And at that moment,
there was a an African-American lady
behind in her car and witnessed
when it happened.
And it was an Afro-American who shot him.
A man.
(Voice raises in pitch.)
From,
what I gather,
from what I heard,
and things,
The gunman
when he was at the stoplight,
the gunman
came up to the car and broke
the driver's side window
and uh
it wasn't one of those distant shots it was a close range,
almost execution style.

ANGELA KING
Rodney King's Aunt

Here's a Nobody

Returning from white iron-gated doorway. To her stool. Heavy pounding rain outside. Day. On her stool, in her studio. Crying, has been crying, prior to the speech for ten minutes straight.

We weren't raised like this.
We weren't raised with no black and white thing.
We were raised with all kinds of friends.
Mexicans, Indians, blacks, whites, Chinese
Most of our friends were Spanish.
Who'd have thought this would happen to us?
Well, I guess there's a first time for everything you know.
(Blowing her nose, she stops crying. A sense in the rest of the speech that she is recovering from a long cry.)
I guess you want me to tell the story
I don't know if you understand sometimes I'm just not in the mood, you know
just not in the mood.
(Slight pause.)
His brother Galen called to say "Cops done beat Glen up!"
Talkin' about Rodney.
I said "What?"
"Police. They got it on tape."
And when I was just turning the channels
I saw this white car.
I heard him holler,
I recognized him layin' there on the ground
that's what got me.
And he looked just like his father too.

Galen was the one used to favor his father.
Now Rodney looks just like him, identical.
I don't know if it's when you lose a life
it comes back in somebody else.
Oh you should have seen him.
It's a hell of a look.
went through three plastic surgeons just to get Rodney to look like
Rodney again.
I tell him he's got a lot
to be thankful for.
A hell of a lot.
He couldn't talk,
just der der der
I said, "Goddamn!"
(Angry.)
My brother's son out there was lookin' like hell
that I saw in that bed and I was gonna fight for every bit of
our justice and fairness.
That (Officer) Koon
that's the one in the whole trial,
that man showed no-kind-of-remorse-at-all,
you know that?
He sit there like "it ain't
no big thing
and I
will do it it *again.*"
And he smile at you.
The nerve,
the audacity!
But I didn't give a damn if it was the President's
whatever it was.
(Slight pause, responding to a question.)
You see how everybody *rave* when something happens with the
President of the United States?
You know, 'cause he's a higher sort?
Okay, here's a nobody.
But the way they beat him.
This is the way I felt towards him.

You understand what I'm sayin' now?
You do? Alright.
(She lights a "More" cigarette, or long brown cigarette.)

THEODORE BRISENO
Police Officer, Acquitted in Beating of Rodney King

Not Their Hero Anymore

With his hands behind his back, cowboy boots. In his lawyer's office.

So it was hard.
Not
only did they look up to me as their father,
I know they looked
at me as their hero.
And that's what
hurt is because
going through all this I felt like,
alright
I'm not their hero anymore.

THE NATIONAL GUARD
COMES TO L.A.

MAXINE WATERS
Congresswoman, 35th District

Washington.

A video of George Bush, Sr. either in Los Angeles, or signing a bill. Dressed like a Congresswoman. Bright suit, scarf, jewelry, impeccable hair, perhaps a wig. At her desk, in her California office. Very enunciated speech.

Oh, Washington
is, um
a place where
ritual and custom
does not allow them,
to,
uh,
talk about things that
don't fit nicely into
the formula.
It's not enough to say they're insensitive,
or they don't care.
They really don't
know.
Not only did they not talk about it,
um,
I had to force myself
on them in every way
and I did.

(Pause, responding to a question.)
I was outrageous
in things that I did. *(She laughs a full, hearty, genuine laugh.)*
When I heard about a meeting at the White House,
to talk about a kind of urban package,
I could not *believe*
that they would *attempt* to even try to *have* this meeting
without involving,
if not me,
the chairman of the Congressional Black Caucus!
If not me,
John Lewis!
Who's supposed to be part of the leadership,
he *is* a *Whip,*
Part of the leadership, right?
I heard about this meeting on *television,*
And when I checked in with the Speaker,
I asked the Speaker if there was a meeting going on.
He said "Yes."
I said, "I was not invited." *("Invited" is enunciated syllable by syllable.)*
Uh.
"Who was invited?"
He said, "It's the leadership.
I don't control the
White House invitations. The President does the inviting
and it's not up to me to decide who's in the meeting."
And I told him,
I said,
"Well,
uh,
what time is this meeting?"
He said, "Well, I'm on my way over there now."
And I said,
"Well, I'll meet you over there,
because," I said,
"I'm coming
over." *(Short laugh.)*
And I was *angry*

and I went out,
I caught a cab.
I drive
but I didn't drive because I didn't trust myself.
I was *angry.*
I caught a cab.
I told the cabdriver, I said,
"Take me to the White House."
I said, "Hurry, I'm late.
I have an appointment at the White House."
He kind of looked at me like,
"Yeah, right."
Some lady inside,
said, "Oh my God, we weren't expecting you."
I said, "You better tell them I'm here."
Someone came out and said, "Right this way,
Congresswoman."
I said, "Thank you."
And the young lady ushered me.
I said,
"Where-is-my-seat?"
And people kind of looked at me,
and I sat down
and everybody sat down
and when the President
came in
everybody stood
and the President looked around the room
and he looked.
When he saw me
he looked,
he had a kind of, quiz
on his face,
but he was nice.
And he went around the room,
and they started to talk about this bill
that was being proposed, the enterprise zone bill,
and after about five or six persons I said,

"Mr. President,
Hi.
I'm here because I want to tell you about what I think is needed
to deal with the serious problem
of unemployment,
hopelessness, and despair
in these cities."
I said, "Los Angeles burned
but Los Angeles is but one
city
experiencing
this kind of hopelessness and despair,"
I said, "and we need a job
program
with stipends … "
I said, "These young people
really,
ya know,
are not in anybody's statistics
or data.
They've been dropped off of everybody's agenda.
They live
from grandmama to mama to girlfriend."
I said,
"We now got young people
who are twenty, twenty-one, twenty-two years old
who have never worked a day of their lives."
I said, "These are the young people in our streets
and they are *angry*
and they are frustrated."
I said, "Don't take my word for it.
Ask Jack Kemp.
Jack Kemp goes, "That's not my
department.
That's better asked of Secretary
Martin."
Well,
Martin was not there, but

her representative
was there
and it turns out
that this was a black man who didn't look black at
all.
He looked at the President
and he said,
"Mr. President,
she's right.
This country is falling
apart."

AFTER DINNER

ALICE WATERS
Chef, Chez Panisse Restaurant, Berkeley, CA

A Civilizing Place

This section is meant to represent a very unlikely dinner party — of people who could never be together. It's after dinner. Dessert and coffee are being served. This would be a good place to cast people according to type, if you have a company of six or more.

It is an elegant dinner party, with an impeccably set table — set by Alice Waters. Table cloth, linen napkins, candles, nice china. Alice Waters is the host.

I just feel like like food
is a way
that that
people can come together.
Everybody has to eat.
And it's something that that
And when you do it well
it has value right you know,
right at the heart of
of it.
When you go buy your bread,
you talk to the baker,
you exchange,
and you feel loyalty,

136

and you go back,
and if something happened to him,
You'd support him
and if something happened to you
he'd help you out.
And when things fell apart in this
country
in the fifties and sixties,
and everything
became processed,
and
Frozen and canned that,
And all of a sudden people had
televisions and
TV dinners
That it just pushed people
away from the table,
and out
into the other rooms.
And that that we we we can't even *begin* to imagine what we've lost,
In that
In that process.
I think we can't uh uh uh
it's just
the table
is really a civilizing place.
It's where a group comes,
and they,
they hear points of view,
they they
they uh
learn about
courtesy and kindness,
uh
they they
learn about
what it is to live in a community.
I think

live in a family first
but live in a bigger community
That's where it comes
Don't you think?

PAUL PARKER*
Chairperson, Free the L.A. Four Plus Defense Committee

Slavery

Dressed differently than before. Golf shirt and slacks.

We spoke out on April twenty-ninth.
It was *some* victory —
I mean it was burnin' *everywhere.*
It was takin' things and nobody was tellin'
Nobody!
It wasn't callin' 911,
"Awww they taken — "
Unh unh it was like, Baby go get some too!
"I'm a little bit too old but get me something — "
You know I mean it was the spirit!
You know they got what?
Eight people?
Eight people?
Out of several thousand?
Um
Um. Um.
They lost!
Oh.
Big Time!
Basically, it's
that you as black people ain't takin' this shit no more.
Even back in slavery.
'Cause I saw *Roots* when I was young.
My dad made sure. He sat us down
in front of that TV
when *Roots* came on,

* *The real Paul Parker appears in a real dinner party seen in the film of* Twilight.

139

so it's embedded in me
since then.
And just to see that Eh, Eh!
This is for Kunta!
This is for Kizzy!
This is for Chicken George!

JIN HO LEE

Seven Names

Heavy accent. Smoking a cigarette. Very expressive.

I don't care if you're black, if you're, uhm, Asian or Caucasian.
And many black people are telling me: "No! We weren't here with
American Dream. We are here as a slave."
I understand.
What I'm saying is, you are not slave at this moment. And I con-
sider their resentment many times, but somehow African-American
people think they are still slave.
That's wrong, that's what's wrong with these people's mind, you
know.
Because, two hundred years ago in Korea, I know if my father was
slave cause there were slaves system in Korea also.
I know because my book telling me I wasn't slave,
I was one of the noble family,
cause we have a history of a family book
that goes back to six hundred years ago. But, what if some of these
people don't have those kind of book,
you know?
Family tree.
We can tell by the name.
There's eight last name that were slave.
Chung, Bao, Chi, Chu, Mah, Wah, Pi …
… oh, seven,
those last names are slaves name, you know.
So you can tell that you were a slave two hundred years ago.
If, if anybody see Mr. Mah, any Korean, he WAS slave.
I mean, their ancestor were slave.
You know, matter a fact my brother-in-law is Mr. Chung.
My grandfather were getting mad because my, my, uh, uh, sister

141

were getting married with the Chung family.

Talking about Korean-Japanese who lives in Korea,

I mean Japan. And their position is very, very similar to African-American

in the United State.

Because they were brought by Japanese from Korea as a slave … in Japan.

And they had to live in Japan as a Korean-Japanese.

Unless they change their name,

they cannot marry the Japanese,

they cannot go to school,

they cannot go to,

they cannot get a job,

because you're Korean.

And there's three things they are good at it: crime, sports, entertainment.

This sounds similar to you, right?

Many famous singers are Korean.

Even the Korean singers who lives in Korea,

many times they go to Japan.

Well we are conquered by Japan,

yeah,

for thirty-six years,

you know?

That's why we,

we brought in Japan as a slaves.

So we know how to,

you know how to feel about this.

I just do not understand that people come up to,

you don't understand how to become slave, you know.

I do!

PAUL PARKER
Chairperson, Free the L.A. Plus Defense Committee

Weapons

They lost seven hundred million dollars.
I was a cornerback,
and I ran some track
and played football,
everything.
I been all off into sports since I was five,
It was
It was bigger than any man type of win I've been involved in
I have so many awards and trophies,
but uhm it's it's *nothing* compared to this!
Now we got some weapons, we got our pride,
we holdin' our heads up and our chest out.
We like yeah brother we did this!
We got the gang truce jumpin' off
We got some weapons ...

ELAINE BROWN
Former Head of the Black Panther Party

Ask Sadaam Hussein

A lot of volume. She stands from the table. Nonstop but rhythmic, easy, rapid, like a poet. A very talented speaker, trained by the oral tradition of the sixties and specifically the oral, verbal life of the Black Panther Party. A member of the Poetry Salon, spoken word movement of the late 1990's, early twenty-first century. Confident, easy, charismatic speech. Recordings are available of her when she was in the Black Panther Party.

Did you know Jonathan Jackson?
Because I did.
And Jonathan Jackson was seventeen years old.
He was probably one of the most brilliant young men,
that you could meet.
He happened to be a science genius.
He was not a gang member by the way.
But Jonathan Jackson
went to a courtroom by himself,
and took over for that one glorious minute
in the name of,
revolution and the freedom of his brother
and other people who were in prison,
and died that day.
My question to you
young brother with a gun in your hand
tough and strong and beautiful as you are,
Do you think it would be better,
if Jonathan Jackson were alive today
or that he died,

that day in Marin County?
Me personally?
I'd rather know Jonathan Jackson.
That's what I'd rather do.
And I'd rather him be alive today
to be among the leadership that we do not have,
than to be dead and in his grave at seventeen years old.
So the question is, how are you going to push the revolutionary
struggle from your grave?
I'm talking merely about strategy
not swashbuckling.
I think that this idea of picking up the gun and going into the
street
without a
plan and without
any more rhyme or reason than rage
is bizarre *(Pronounced Bee-zarre.)* and so uh *(Takes out a Gitanes
and smokes.)*
and it's foolish
because it will uh
I think that
all one has to do
is ask to ask the Vietnamese,
or Sadaam Hussein
about the power and weaponry,
and arsenal of the United States government and its willingness to
use it,
to get to understanding what this is about.
You are not facing a
you know, some little Nicaraguan clique
here.
You are not in Havana in nineteen-fifty something.
This is the United States of America.
There isn't another *country,*
there isn't another *community,*
that is more organized and armed.
It is not only naive
uh

it is foolish if one is talking
about jumping out into the street,
and waving a gun,
and so forth and so on and doing that "bad" thing.
Because you not that bad.
you see what I'm saying?
You just not that bad.
You *think* you bad
but I say again,
ask Sadaam Hussein
about who is bad
and you'll get the answer.
So what I'm saying is
Be conscious of what you are doing.
If you just want to *die*
and become a poster
go ahead and do that.
We will all put you on the wall with all the rest of the people,
But if you want to effect change for your people,
and you are serious about it
(That doesn't mean throw down your gun
matter of fact I would def definitely never tell anybody to do that
not black and in America)
But if you are talking about *a war*
against the United States govment.
Then you better talk to Sadaam Hussein
and you better talk to the Vietnamese people,
and the Nicaraguan,
and El Salvadorans,
and people in South Africa,
and people in other countries in Southeast Asia,
and ask those motherfuckers,
what this country is capable of doing!
So all I am saying is,
if you are committed,
if you seriously make a commitment
because,
and that commitment

must be based not on hate but on *love*.
And that's the other thing,
my theme is
that *love* of your people
then you gon' have to realize that this may have to be a lifetime
commitment
and that the longer you live
the more you can do!
So don't get hung up
on your own ego,
and your own image,
and pumping up your muscles,
and putting on a black beret,
or some kinda Malcolm X hat or whatever other
regalia
and symbolic vestment you can put on your body
Think in terms of what
are you going to do
for black people.
I'm saying that these
are the long-haul.
Because *then* you might be talkin' about
bein' in a better position for a so-called
armed-struggle.
At this point you talking about a *piss-poor*
rag-tag unorganized *poorly armed*
and *poorly poorly*
uh uhm
poorly *led*
army
and it's not going to uhn, ih
we just be thrown back
and we will be twenty more years
trying to figure out what happened to Martin, Malcolm
and the Black Panther Party.

PAUL PARKER
Chairperson, Free the L.A. Four Plus Defense Committee

In a Way That Was Just

Pausing, responding to her.

We just spoke out
We didn't have a plan
We just acted, and we acted in a way that was just.

BILL BRADLEY
Former Senator, D-New Jersey

You're Being Held Against Your Will, Aren't You?

Expensive shoes, coat, tie. Easy speech, used to talking, giving speeches. Reasoned.

One of the things that strike me about,
uh, the events of Los Angeles, for example, was, um, the following:
I have a friend
an African-American
uh, was, uhhh,
I think a second year Harvard Law school student.
And he was interning
a summer in the late seventies
out in LA, at a big law firm,
and every Sunday
the ... different partners would ...
would invite the interns to their home
for tea or brunch or whatever.
And this was a particular Sunday and he was on his way driving
to one of the partner's homes.
There's a white woman in the car with him.
I think she was an intern.
I'm not positive of that.
They were driving and they were in the very ...
just about the neighborhood of the,
uh, partner, obviously well-to-do neighborhood in Los Angeles.
Suddenly he looks in the rearview mirror.
There is a, uh, police car,
red light.
He pulls over.
Police cars pull in front of him.

149

Police jump out,
guns, pull him out of the car,
throw him to the floor
put a handcuff on him behind his back.
All the while pointing a gun at him. *(Rapid, he performs this, ges-
turing the gun down to the floor)*
Run around to the woman on the other side. "You're being held
against your will, aren't you, being held against your will."
She gets hysterical,
and they keep their guns pointed.
Takes them fifteen or twenty minutes to convince them
"No, no. I'm not, uh, I'm not, uh, I'm, I'm, I'm, I'm an intern, law
firm,
I'm on my way to a meeting, partner's *brunch.*"
And after that, he convinces them of that, while his head is down in
the ground, right?
They take the handcuffs off.
They say, "Okay, go ahead."
They put their hats on, flip their sunglasses down, get in their
police
cars, and drive away, as if nothing happened.
So my first reaction
to that is, um …
The events of April aren't new
or the Rodney King
episode isn't news in Los Angeles
or in many other places.
My second thought is: What did the partner of that law firm do on
Monday?
Did the partner call the police commissioner?
Did the partner call anybody?
The answer is no.
And it gets to, well,
who's got a responsibility here?

RUDY SALAS
Sculptor and Painter

How Do You Think a Father Feels?

More dressed up than earlier.

I had a lot of anxieties about my boys.
Stephen was at Stanford!
Came home one weekend to sing with the band!
Cop pulled him over!
pulled a gun at his head!
How do you think a father feels?
Stuff that happened to me
Fifty years ago, happening to my sons, man!
They didn't tell me
because it would make me sick!
it would make me sick!

PAUL PARKER
Chairperson, Free the L.A. Four Plus Defense Committee

What I'm Doing for, Say, Justice

If I don't do what I'm doing for, say, justice
when I do
happen to die,
pass away,
I won't be able to really rest,
I won't have no peace,
'cause I didn't do something in terms of justice.

BILL BRADLEY
Senator, D-New Jersey

Application of the Laws

Speaks very rapidly.

I mean, all of us have responsibility
to try to improve the circumstances
among the races of this country.
I mean, you know, uh, a teenage mother's got a responsibility,
to realize that if she has more children the life chances of those
children are gonna be *less;*
The gang member's gotta be held accountable for his finger on a gun.
Right?
The corporate executive has gotta be responsible for hiring and
promoting diverse talent.
And the head of the law firm's gotta be responsible for that as well.
But,
both the corporate executive and the law firm have to use their
moral power.
If that's not a total contradiction.
I don't think it is.
The *moral power* of the law firm,
or corporation when
moments arise such as my friends' face in the ground with the gun
pointed at his head because he was in the wrong neighborhood and
black.
And the moral power, of those institutions have to be brought to
bear
in the public institutions, which in many places are not *fair!*
To put it mildly.
Right? And the *application* of the law
before which we are all in *theory* equal.

ALICE WATERS
Chef, Chez Panisse Restaurant, Berkeley, CA

Marching Orders

I think there are a lot of people
from my generation
and younger people.
People are
we're all waiting,
to have an opport ...
To get those marching orders,
we're all waiting!
Just tell me
Where is the show?
What do I have to do?
Just
help organize me,
so that I can participate!
We don't have the leaders.
Why don't we have the leaders?
Because people
haven't been asked to
step up in that way.
It's true
We're all waiting
to help
but we just don't know how to.
It's so *big*
And it's happening so quickly.
And-we-need-to-stop-
what's-happening.
And pretty soon you realize that
what's happening out there,
with the kids in the streets

is is/you know it's
my problem
and what's happening in the schools,
is um
has to do with
the future
of our
our kids
And I just feel like the
best way to influence those
kids is to
help educate them in the public school
system
And to teach them to open their senses.
Do you know that eighty-five precent of kids
in this country
Don't eat one meal with their family
a day?
I think uh uh I think we just
forgot um, you know
it just got thrown out that idea of being around a table.
And we don't know what got
thrown out
with it
and, uh, there are a lot of things that happen around a table
even if you don't *like* what's on the table
and you don't li —
and if you can't communicate with your family,
you have to sit there in a way,
and wait 'til that guy stops talking so that you go
pass the bread to another
or use a napkin or a fork or a knife.
And those things are becoming very foreign to a lot of children!
It's an *offering*
to-someone-who-needs-food
It's *healing*
And I think that's what the table is!
It's an offering to nourish people!

And the more you're out there
The more you realize
what's upstream is coming downstream.
The more you realize
that
you know
we're all
sort of connected here.
(She blows out the candles, but the table stays upstage of the action that follows.)

JUSTICE

MARIA
Juror #7, Federal Trial

AA Meeting

*African American, sexy, high heeled shoes. She "acts out" all
of the characters she refers to physically as well as vocally. She
is a good mimic.*

Just to show you how we came up with the verdict,
So we get in there,
and we say let's get with the evidence.
And we got to about half the testimonies,
Cause we started with Powell,
and it was leading so much towards guilty.
And somebody says, "Wait a minute wait a minute,
let's stop
I am tired
I think what we should do
we should color code our book
let's take the day off and let's color code our books."
You know, how in our books we have
we put a green tab,
so if somebody says
"I wanna hear Melanie Singer then we can find Melanie
Singer"
Okay, so we spend a whole day doing that.
Then the next day
things are going good.
And somebody says

"Oh man,
I'm tired
I'm really tired
I think we should quit for the day and start tomorrow
I just can't take it no more.
It's just too much on my head,"
Okay,
so I'm thinkin' alright,
I know what they doin' cause every time we quit,
we go back another step.
And you're not allowed to talk about the case outside,
but we're human
so people would talk,
but they would talk about personal feelings
and that's not talking about the trial that's talking about the person?
At breakfast,
sometimes
like,
I mean "Look at Rodney King.
Why should we spend all this money
for a man like that?"
To me what they're saying
"This man,
he did this to a police officer,
why should we spend all this money
for someone like that?"
And they kept talking about he had a parole hold,
that stuff didn't have anything,
to do with the case.
The case was
was-his-civil-rights-violated.
It was not,
what kind of man
Rodney King
was or,
what kind of man
the defendants were —
So this stuff —

it didn't come up in court
so it shouldn't be comin' up in this breakfast room!
So then,
we quit again
we come back the next day.
And so we're goin' through the evidence,
and this lady says,
"Oh my God, I think, I'm getting a headache.
I think I'm getting a headache
I think I'm getting brain dead
Let's just quit"
I said "Wait a minute!"
I don't want to go to the hotel.
There's nothing to do there!
I said I hate goin' there
I don't wanna go back.
I wanna stay here!"
So the foreman says "Okay,
let's just stay here and everybody can do what they
want
so we do what we want."
So the next day I'm *pissed*
Because every time we get right-here,
someone is brain dead,
or someone is tired, or someone has a headache.
So we get back in.
And I'm arguing with this one guy on this PCP and he is saying —
stupid stuff that didn't have,
anything to do with the case.
And I said
"Wait a minute
I do not trust you!
I do not trust your judgment!
You're bull crappin' with me right now.
I said ON THIS BOOK IT SAYS THIS!"
So somebody says
"Now wait a minute Maria,
Calm down

Why don't you trust him?
What's the matter."
I said "I heard the comments that's going around,"
I said "It's not being directed towards me.
What do you mean,
Why should we go through a case like this for a man like that?
If you felt that way you should have told the judge that at the
beginning.
You should not be bringing that up here!"
He looks at me and he turns really really red.
Now the *black* guy jumps up
"Maria I think you just being too sensitive
'bout this thing
the man was just playin'
we been jokin' since we been here
and you have no right
to talk to him like that,"
and that just broke me.
Because I didn't expect that to come from him
and that gave everybody else reason to jump on me
and people are like,
"Yeah you're just stirring up shit!"
So I got up and I went to bathroom and cry.
So I'm washing my face
so I stayed in the bathroom
and I tried to came out all strong
and I tried to smile
and when I came out
and they all hugged me
and "Oh, we're so sorry we didn't mean it!"
and now they're really being sincere with me.
Except the black guy he didn't apologize right?
and the guy who yelled at me
He's crying,
and he said
"I just want to say one thing
I marched in the *Martin Luther King March!*
and I'm sittin' there like,

I didn't even know what that meant.
And after this day
everybody was so different towards
me
there was no whispering your name,
it was ...
Now at this point that,
I broke down
everybody trusted me as a person
right?
And now
Everyone is coming out of their *prejudice!*
The next day
is when we had our AA
meeting,
oh God when you hear it,
You gonna say "My God."
After that breakdown that I had,
no one
couldn't sleep.
I'm serious.
And we're back in the jury room.
And
the Foreman Steve raises his hand,
and he says
"I just want everybody to know,
I called
Alice a asshole."
And so Alice
raises her hand
"I really don't think that's fair that you called me a asshole like that
and I think you should apologize to me in front of everybody
it's just really not fair."
And Steve raises his hand,
cause mind you we raise our hand to keep everything in order
and Steve says
"I just want you guys to know,
that my intentions was not,

to apologize to Alice
that was not my intentions,
I just wanted everybody to know that *I did call her a asshole*
at breakfast today."
So this one guy says
"I think you guys should air out your differences at the hotel."
Here come Steve
"Let me tell you some-
thing.
First of all I don't respect Alice!
and if I get one inch near her,
I'm gonna knock her fuckin' head off!"
and Alice's like
"I'm writing to the judge
I just got threatened for my life."
Here come Steve
"I will not
hit you
Alice.
I don't respect you, but I won't hit you"
Here come the Mexican guy
"I just want to say if anybody wants to hit
me they can hit me,
I'm free for any punches that might go on."
So this guy raises his hand
"You know I just feel like,
I agree with Maria."
'Cause at the beginning I had said
told everybody that I don't think they're telling the truth when they
say they're tired
'Cause I said
"I work at the Post Office!
They tell me I got two hours of overtime, after I worked eight hours,
I'm tired too,
but
I don't go home!
and I still stay there,
and I do a damn good job at it,

and I said
"This is our job
and we are not tired!"
So this guy says "I agree with Maria!"
And he's like a younger guy
He says "I told you guys,
don't be pussying around here!
And if you're fucking tired,
then
take your asses home
we have *three alternates* that would like to take your places
so get your asses out if you're tired."
Then the black guy stands up
"Let me tell you something
I have not slept,
in two weeks, do you hear me?
two weeks I have been in here
And I have not had one bit of sleep,
I have broken out in hives!"
And he pulls his shirt off and he is like *red* all over
just hives all over his body!
"And I don't appreciate you … "
And he breaks out crying
and I thought the man was gonna die and have a heart attack,
so he cries really hard and he runs out
and this real high class lady who was over on the side
doing like this
(Paces in circle shaking hands.)
saying "I hate arguing. I hate arguing"
She jumps in and she starts crying
"Oh please if anybody writes a book
if anybody makes a movie,
please don't nobody
please don't say nothin' about my family."
Such and such,
and she starts talking about something in her family
confessing it
we had no idea about it

why is she telling us now?
"Please please don't tell it in the movie"
So now the black guy
got rushed off to the hospital
cause he was about to have a heart attack.
But after that
day
which you noticed, everybody broke
this stuff didn't have nothing to do with the trial,
But what happened was everybody came out of their prejudice
their feelings about the defendants,
their guilty,
whatever they thought inside that was guilty,
that they had on their minds,
I'm saying that peoples *personal* guilts
their personal beliefs
got put aside.
And it was washed away.
Once they took that away
we were able to look at the evidence,
the testimony,
without bringing up what happened to my sister
a long time ago.
Right after that
we came to the verdict like that.
(She snaps her fingers.)
The verdict on Powell
was *guilty*
No one cried.
No one argued.
We just went through the evidence
okay such and such said this
just like we were in school.
It was like simple boom, boom, boom.
We was finished with Powell that day.
It took us five days,
four and a half days,
to get to that AA meeting?

After that AA meeting it took us two days to come up with a verdict for all
four of 'em.

MRS. YOUNG-SOON HAN
Former Liquor Store Owner

Swallowing the Bitterness

At a low coffee table. Deep voice.

When I was in Korea,
I used to watch many luxurious Hollywood lifestyle movies.
I never saw any poor man,
any black
maybe one housemaid?
Until last year
I believed America is the best.
I still believe it.
I don't deny that now.
Because I'm victim.
But
as
the year ends in ninety-two,
and we were still in turmoil,
and having all the financial problems,
and mental problems,
then a couple months ago,
I really realized that
Korean immigrants were left out
from this
society and we were nothing.
What is our right?
Is it because we are Korean?
Is it because we have no politicians?
Is it because we don't
speak good English?
Why?

Why do we have to be left out?
(She is hitting her hand on the coffee table.)
We are not qualified to have medical treatment!
We are not qualified to get uh
food stamps!
(She hits the table once.)
No GR!
(Hits the table once.)
No welfare!
(Hits the table once.)
Anything!
Many Afro-Americans
(Two quick hits.)
who never worked
(One hit.)
they get
at least minimum amount
(One hit.)
of money
(One hit.)
to survive!
(One hit.)
We don't get any!
(Large hit with full hand spread.)
Because we have a *car!*
(One hit.)
and we have a *house!*
(Pause six seconds.)
And we are *high tax payers!*
(One hit.)
(Pause fourteen seconds.)
Where do I finda [sic] justice?
Okay, black people
Probably,
believe they won
by the trial?
Even some complains only half, right
justice was there?

But I watched the television
that Sunday morning
Early morning as they started
I started watch it all day.
They were having party, and then they celebrated *(Pronounced
CeLEbreted.)*
all of South Central,
all the churches,
they finally found that justice exists
in this society.
Then where is the victims' rights?
They got their rights
by destroying *innocent Korean merchants (Louder.)*
They have a lot of respect, *(Softer.)*
as I do
for Dr. Martin King?
He is the only model for black community.
I don't care Jesse Jackson.
But,
he was the model
of non-violence
Non-violence?
They like to have hiseh [sic] spirits.
What about last year?
They destroyed innocent people!
(Five second pause.)
And I wonder if that is really justice,
(And a very soft uh after justice like justicah, but very quick.)
to get their rights
in this way.
(Thirteen second pause.)
I waseh swallowing the bitternesseh.
Sitting here alone, and watching them.
They became all hilarious.
(Three second pause.)
And uh,
in a way I was happy for them,
and I felt glad for them,

at least they got something back, you know.
Just lets forget Korean victims or other victims
who are destroyed by them.
They have fought
for their rights
(One hit simultaneous with the word rights.)
over two centuries
(One hit simultaneous with centuries.)
and I have a lot of sympathy and understanding for them.
Because of their effort, and sacrificing,
other minorities like And Hispanic
or Asians
maybe we have to suffer more
by mainstream,
you know?
That's why I understand.
And then
I like to be part of their
joyment.
But.
That's why I had mixed feeling
as soon as I heard the verdict.
I wish I could
live together
with eh [sic] blacks
but after the riots
there were too much differences
The fire is still there
how do you call it
*(She says a Korean word asking for translation. In Korean, she says
"igniting fire.")*
igni
igniting fire
It canuh
burst out any time.

TWILIGHT

TWILIGHT BEY
Organizer, Gang Truce

Limbo

Walking the full stage and around the table from the dinner party.

So a lot of times when I've brought up ideas to my homeboys,
They say
"Twilight
that's before your time
that's something you can't do now."
When I talked about the truce back in 1988,
that was something they considered before its time.
Yet
in 1992,
we made it
realistic.
So to me, it's like I'm stuck in limbo,
like the sun is stuck between night and day,
in the twilight hours,
You know?
I'm in an area not many people exist.
Night time to me
is like a lack of sun.
And I don't affiliate
darkness with anything negative.
I affiliate
darkness of what was first

because it *was first*
and then relative to my complexion,
I am a *dark* individual,
and with me stuck in limbo
I see the darkness as myself
I see the light *(He lights a candle.)* as knowledge and the wisdom
of the world and understanding others.
And in order for me to be, a to be, a true human being.
I can't forever dwell in darkness.
I can't forever dwell in the idea,
just identifying with people like me, and understanding me and
mine.
So twilight
is
that time
between day and night
limbo
I call it limbo.
(He blows out the candle and walks off the stage.)

End of Play

PROPERTY LIST

British-made ottoman, tea (JESSYE NORMAN)
High stool (ANGELA KING)
More cigarettes (ANGELA KING, CORNEL WEST)
Gitanes cigarette (ELAINE BROWN)
Cigarette (JIN HO LEE)
Wedding ring (STANLEY K. SHEINBAUM)
Table (RUDY SALAS, SR., SERGEANT CHARLES DUKE, KEITH WATSON, OCTAVIO SANDOVAL, ELVIRA EVERS, SHELBY COFFEY III, CORNEL WEST, ELAINE BROWN, MRS. YOUNG-SOON HAN, ALICE WATERS, TWILIGHT BEY)
Stool or chair (SHELBY COFFEY III, KATIE MILLER)
Piece of cement (looks like sculpture) (SHELBY COFFEY III, KEITH WATSON)
Plastic table cloth, large bottle of Pepsi, hearing aid (RUDY SALAS, SR.)
Eyeglasses (RUDY SALAS, SR., ANONYMOUS MAN / JUROR IN SIMI VALLEY TRIAL, JOE VIOLA)
Drinking glass (RUDY SALAS, SR., SERGEANT CHARLES DUKE)
Desk (ELAINE YOUNG, KEITH WATSON, CHARLES LLOYD, GINA RAE AKA QUEEN MALKAH)
Large metal watch, cash register (JAY WOONG YAHNG)
Fancy eyeglasses, paper cup of coffee in a bag, sweet and lows, silver plated pen, large fancy leather-bound photo album (ELAINE YOUNG)
Phone (ELAINE YOUNG, ANONYMOUS TALENT AGENT)
Two red boxing gloves, remote, fine furnishings (CHARLES LLOYD)
Television (CHARLES LLOYD, SERGEANT CHARLES DUKE)
Expensive desk accessories (ELAINE YOUNG, CHARLES LLOYD, ANONYMOUS TALENT AGENT)
Policeman's baton, pitcher of water, rolling cart for television (SERGEANT CHARLES DUKE)

Lamp on a timer (ANONYMOUS MAN /JUROR IN SIMI
    VALLEY TRIAL)
Comfortable armchair (ANONYMOUS MAN /JUROR IN
    SIMI VALLEY TRIAL, CORNEL WEST)
Cheese and crackers (JOE VIOLA)
Baby bottle (ELVIRA EVERS)
Lamp, Cognac and snifter (CORNEL WEST)
Large daytime organizer, keys (REGINALD DENNY)
Pencil, legal pad (PAUL PARKER)
Dessert, coffee, table cloth, linen napkins, nice china (ALICE
    WATERS)
Candles (ALICE WATERS, TWILIGHT BEY)

SOUND EFFECTS

Bird chirps loudly
Intercom beeps
Little child says, "Mommy"
Baby making noise
Bell rings
Sounds of birds and a lawn mower
Sounds of a riot
Police sirens
Buildings on fire
Hip hop, rap music
Helicopters
Chants
Gunshots

NEW PLAYS

★ **AFTER ASHLEY by Gina Gionfriddo.** A teenager is unwillingly thrust into the national spotlight when a family tragedy becomes talk-show fodder. "A work that virtually any audience would find accessible." *–NY Times.* "Deft characterization and caustic humor." *–NY Sun.* "A smart satirical drama." *–Variety.* [4M, 2W] ISBN: 978-0-8222-2099-2

★ **THE RUBY SUNRISE by Rinne Groff.** Twenty-five years after Ruby struggles to realize her dream of inventing the first television, her daughter faces similar battles of faith as she works to get Ruby's story told on network TV. "Measured and intelligent, optimistic yet clear-eyed." *–NY Magazine.* "Maintains an exciting sense of ingenuity." *–Village Voice.* "Sinuous theatrical flair." *–Broadway.com.* [3M, 4W] ISBN: 978-0-8222-2140-1

★ **MY NAME IS RACHEL CORRIE taken from the writings of Rachel Corrie, edited by Alan Rickman and Katharine Viner.** This solo piece tells the story of Rachel Corrie who was killed in Gaza by an Israeli bulldozer set to demolish a Palestinian home. "Heartbreaking urgency. An invigoratingly detailed portrait of a passionate idealist." *–NY Times.* "Deeply authentically human." *–USA Today.* "A stunning dramatization." *–CurtainUp.* [1W] ISBN: 978-0-8222-2222-4

★ **ALMOST, MAINE by John Cariani.** This charming midwinter night's dream of a play turns romantic clichés on their ear as it chronicles the painfully hilarious amorous adventures (and misadventures) of residents of a remote northern town that doesn't quite exist. "A whimsical approach to the joys and perils of romance." *–NY Times.* "Sweet, poignant and witty." *–NY Daily News.* "Aims for the heart by way of the funny bone." *–Star-Ledger.* [2M, 2W] ISBN: 978-0-8222-2156-2

★ **Mitch Albom's TUESDAYS WITH MORRIE by Jeffrey Hatcher and Mitch Albom, based on the book by Mitch Albom.** The true story of Brandeis University professor Morrie Schwartz and his relationship with his student Mitch Albom. "A touching, life-affirming, deeply emotional drama." *–NY Daily News.* "You'll laugh. You'll cry." *–Variety.* "Moving and powerful." *–NY Post.* [2M] ISBN: 978-0-8222-2188-3

★ **DOG SEES GOD: CONFESSIONS OF A TEENAGE BLOCKHEAD by Bert V. Royal.** An abused pianist and a pyromaniac ex-girlfriend contribute to the teen-angst of America's most hapless kid. "A welcome antidote to the notion that the *Peanuts* gang provides merely American cuteness." *–NY Times.* "Hysterically funny." *–NY Post.* "The *Peanuts* kids have finally come out of their shells." *–Time Out.* [4M, 4W] ISBN: 978-0-8222-2152-4

DRAMATISTS PLAY SERVICE, INC.
440 Park Avenue South, New York, NY 10016 212-683-8960 Fax 212-213-1539
postmaster@dramatists.com   www.dramatists.com

NEW PLAYS

★ **RABBIT HOLE by David Lindsay-Abaire.** Winner of the 2007 Pulitzer Prize. Becca and Howie Corbett have everything a couple could want until a life-shattering accident turns their world upside down. "An intensely emotional examination of grief, laced with wit." *—Variety.* "A transcendent and deeply affecting new play." *—Entertainment Weekly.* "Painstakingly beautiful." *—BackStage.* [2M, 3W] ISBN: 978-0-8222-2154-8

★ **DOUBT, A Parable by John Patrick Shanley.** Winner of the 2005 Pulitzer Prize and Tony Award. Sister Aloysius, a Bronx school principal, takes matters into her own hands when she suspects the young Father Flynn of improper relations with one of the male students. "All the elements come invigoratingly together like clockwork." *—Variety.* "Passionate, exquisite, important, engrossing." *—NY Newsday.* [1M, 3W] ISBN: 978-0-8222-2219-4

★ **THE PILLOWMAN by Martin McDonagh.** In an unnamed totalitarian state, an author of horrific children's stories discovers that someone has been making his stories come true. "A blindingly bright black comedy." *—NY Times.* "McDonagh's least forgiving, bravest play." *—Variety.* "Thoroughly startling and genuinely intimidating." *—Chicago Tribune.* [4M, 5 bit parts (2M, 1W, 1 boy, 1 girl)] ISBN: 978-0-8222-2100-5

★ **GREY GARDENS book by Doug Wright, music by Scott Frankel, lyrics by Michael Korie.** The hilarious and heartbreaking story of Big Edie and Little Edie Bouvier Beale, the eccentric aunt and cousin of Jacqueline Kennedy Onassis, once bright names on the social register who became East Hampton's most notorious recluses. "An experience no passionate theatergoer should miss." *—NY Times.* "A unique and unmissable musical." *—Rolling Stone.* [4M, 3W, 2 girls] ISBN: 978-0-8222-2181-4

★ **THE LITTLE DOG LAUGHED by Douglas Carter Beane.** Mitchell Green could make it big as the hot new leading man in Hollywood if Diane, his agent, could just keep him in the closet. "Devastatingly funny." *—NY Times.* "An out-and-out delight." *—NY Daily News.* "Full of wit and wisdom." *—NY Post.* [2M, 2W] ISBN: 978-0-8222-2226-2

★ **SHINING CITY by Conor McPherson.** A guilt-ridden man reaches out to a therapist after seeing the ghost of his recently deceased wife. "Haunting, inspired and glorious." *—NY Times.* "Simply breathtaking and astonishing." *—Time Out.* "A thoughtful, artful, absorbing new drama." *—Star-Ledger.* [3M, 1W] ISBN: 978-0-8222-2187-6

DRAMATISTS PLAY SERVICE, INC.
440 Park Avenue South, New York, NY 10016 212-683-8960 Fax 212-213-1539
postmaster@dramatists.com www.dramatists.com